Classic ITALIAN C·U·I·S·I·N·E

Edited by Rosemary Moon

TIGER BOOKS INTERNATIONAL
LONDON

ILLUSTRATIONS BY
CAMILLA SOPWITH AND LAWRIE TAYLOR

CLB 4363
This edition published 1995 by
Tiger Books International PLC, Twickenham
© 1995 CLB Publishing, Godalming, Surrey
Typeset by SX Composing, Rayleigh, Essex
All rights reserved
Printed and bound in South Africa
ISBN 1-85501-616-8

CONTENTS

INTRODUCTION 8

SOUPS & STARTERS 22

VEGETABLES & SALADS 40

LIGHT LUNCHES & SUPPER DISHES 64

RICE, PIZZAS & PANCAKES 104

FISH 128

CHICKEN & VEAL 162

MEAT & GAME 186

DESSERTS, ICES & BISCUITS 216

INDEX 250

INTRODUCTION

There are basically two types of Italian cookbooks. One is lavishly illustrated with glorious colour photographs, often of landscapes and scenes that will remind you of holidays past, or encourage you in the planning of holidays to come. The other is more practical, relying on the tastebuds to inspire you to culinary delights. This book is of the second type. It does not dwell on regional cooking, despite the fact that Italy is a fiercely regional country, but is a general introduction to the delights of classic Italian cuisine.

Italian cookery is amongst the best in the world. It is steeped in tradition and we know for a fact that the Italians have been experimenting with local and imported foodstuffs for 2,000 years or more. The earliest known cookbook, dating from the first century BC, is Roman, and many of our staple foods can be traced back to this time and beyond. Throughout the culinary history of Europe it is easy to see the influence of the Roman Empire – the way in which the Roman soldiers took their favourite foods with them on the their travels, and then returned home with the best produce from their newly conquered outposts and territories.

Italy itself is long and thin – the boot-shaped piece of Europe that hangs out into the Mediterranean Sea. It is one of the first countries that children learn to recognise, easily identified by its own distinctive shape, and that of the two large islands of Sardinia and Sicily, the latter forming a ball or rock to be kicked by the boot-shape of the Italian mainland. The influence of modern Italian cookery and the spread of popular pasta dishes and pizzas, could mean that children throughout Europe will soon be accepting some classic Italian foods almost as part of their own culinary heritage.

A Recent Blending of Cultures

So much more has been written about Ancient Rome than the other cities and regions around it. This may be because many cultures were absorbed into Rome and the one city came to dominate the early history of Italy and, indeed, of much of Europe. Italy is only recently united – the country that we know, with the current borders and boundaries, has only been recognised for a century or so. Before that, it was a series of city states, all fiercely proud of their traditions and independence and, indeed, of their regional cooking skills. These states were often at war with each other and, to this day, maintain their pride in their past traditions. So, Italian cookery today is a combination of many regional skills and specialities.

Ancient Rome – the Kitchen of Europe

The facts pertaining to daily life in Ancient Rome are more accessible than those concerning wars and the establishment of the Roman community. This is simply because the legends of Ancient Rome were handed down by mouth or reported from one country to another with the inevitable verbal embellishments, to the extent that Roman scholars really don't know what is or isn't true, unless they have some actual proof in the way of buildings or wall paintings, for example. The tales of gluttony and Bacchanalian orgies in Rome may well have been exaggerated, although we do know that banquets and feasts in the ancient world were pretty incredible in both their size and duration.

The Founding of Rome

The founding of Rome is attributed to Romulus and Remus, twin brothers from Alba Longa, a nearby city. The brothers founded the city, built on seven hills, in 753 BC and were its first rulers. However, they are said to have brought in prisoners of war from other cities and states and the ancient people of Rome were probably from three tribes or peoples, the Latins, the Sabines from mountainous country east of the River Tiber, and Etruscans from the coastal region to the north of Rome, now known as Tuscany. Whatever the origin of the Roman people, there is no doubt that they worked hard together and developed many things that are now part of everyday modern life, for example central heating or, with more relevance to culinary tradition, the first bread ovens.

By 264 BC Rome had dominated and conquered most of the Italian peninsular and set about capturing its first overseas target – Sicily. This was won from Carthage in 242 BC – the Romans had a long struggle to learn domination of the seas – and Sardinia and Corsica were taken as provinces soon afterwards. From then on the Roman Empire grew and grew, eventually spreading throughout Europe and including areas of the Middle East and North Africa, all of which, in their turn, contributed to the culinary inheritance of Rome and Italy in general.

Coffee Drinking – a Great Italian Tradition

Think of Italy, think of a drink and you will probably think of wine for Italy is, with France, Europe's largest producer of grapes and wine. However, Italy made a significant contribution to the drinking habits of Europe in the sixteenth century through the popularisation of coffee drinking.

Legend has it that coffee was first drunk by a goatherd in the Yemen, who found that boiling the beans with water produced a liquor that would keep him awake through the night whilst tending his flock. Coffee was thus an established drink in Arab lands, especially in the eastern Mediterranean, for many years before it became popular throughout Europe.

In 1585 the Venetian Ambassador to Turkey reported back on the Turkish habit of drinking a black water that kept them awake called *cavee*. Coffee was subsequently imported into Italy through the port of Venice and coffee shops quickly became popular. These soon spread throughout Europe – an Italian nick-named Procope introduced both coffee and the great Italian delicacies of ice creams and granitas to Paris, and thus to France, through his coffee shop in the Rue de l'Ancienne Comédie, which is still there, bearing his name.

Italian coffee is regarded by many as the best. It is strong because of the very high roasting of the beans. When I owned a delicatessen and lined up the coffee jars, the Italian roast was always at one end of the display containing the blackest and most pungent beans.

Espresso and Cappuccino are the two most popular types of Italian coffee. Espresso is usually served in demi-tasse or small cups and is always drunk black. It is strong and slightly bitter, an excellent reviver after a heavy meal or a late night. My personal favourite is the cappuccino which is traditionally only drunk in the mornings, more as a breakfast coffee. It is topped with a creamy froth and dredged with cocoa powder – it is difficult to make a good cappuccino at home as a machine is required for the froth. The easiest way to make good Italian coffee is by using a pot called a napolentana, which allows hot water to percolate through the ground coffee into an earthenware pot – it is used on the hob and, once mastered, many people would never consider any other method of coffee making. Iced coffee is also very popular in Italy and is very refreshing – it is interesting that, like iced tea, it has never really become popular in the UK.

Olive Oil – an Ancient Currency...

Italy is currently one of the leading producers of olive oil and the town of Lucca, north of Pisa in Tuscany, is regarded as the centre of the Italian olive oil trade. However, in the days of Ancient Rome, the olive oil that was sold in the Trajan Forum, the first food market built around 150 BC, was imported from Spain. Olive oil was a valuable trading commodity and was as highly prized in ancient times as it is today. I can find no record of when the first olives were actually grown in Italy but they were originally native to the eastern Mediterranean and are likely to have spread throughout the whole region long before the time of Christ.

...and a Modern Commodity

Interest in olive oil has never been greater than it is today. Originally an ingredient for gourmets only outside the countries of the Mediterranean, it has been in constant use by the people of Italy and the other Mediterranean lands for centuries but has really only just received recognition in less temperate climates. Even 30 years ago the oil was considered to be a luxury in England by all but the most ardent cooks (a tiny bottle was kept in the medicine cupboard in our house when I was a child!) but now it is available to all at a reasonable price.

Modern technology has certainly helped the production of olive oil and almost all producers (with the possible exception of the smallest farmers making oil only for their local community) now use centrifugal presses, leading to a much better extraction rate and, therefore, a more affordable oil. Italy now produces around 468,000 metric tons of olive oil a year and 2.3 million metric tons of olives.

The Production of Olive Oil

There are three grades of olive oil, categorised according to acidity. The very best is the extra virgin, usually dark green in colour and fruity in flavour, with an acidity of less than 1 per cent. Virgin oils are similar in colour and have an acidity below 4 per cent, while the cheapest and most mass produced oils, often yellow and sometimes taken from the olives during a second extraction, have less character and are frequently blended. Up until 1991 such oils were described as pure – well, that was slightly misleading as it sounded so grand!

Olives tend to be grown either for the table or for their oil. One of the most romantic sights of the Mediterranean for me is the wizened trunks of the olive trees supporting branches heavily laden with fruits. Do not be tempted in a moment of romantic madness to pluck an olive from a branch for your loved one – they are perfectly disgusting until they have been steeped in a mild pickling solution! Olives are either harvested green or black but they are the same fruit – the black (actually a dark red when picked) have merely been left to ripen, in the same way that red peppers are ripe green ones!

The olives are harvested by shaking the trees over nets which catch the fruit. Mechanical picking would damage them as would heavy-handed manual picking so the time-honoured method of tree shaking is by far the best. Olives for oil production are then crushed, allowing the oil to seep from the pulp. This is traditionally known as cold pressing. However, all large factories and serious producers now use centrifugal presses, which lacerate and spin the olives achieving a much higher extraction rate than the more traditional methods at the first pressing. Any remaining oil is then extracted by heating the mulch to allow the oil to flow more freely, thus producing a more refined and less flavoursome oil. The advent of the centrifugal press has certainly brought the virgin and extra virgin olive oils to within the financial reach of most keen cooks – hurrah for progress (well, in this case)!

A Tasting Language for Oils

Demand leads supply and the current high interest in cookery has certainly led to a willingness to experiment with different oils in the kitchen. Delicatessens and specialist food shops have long stocked a wide variety of oils, not only from Italy but from all around the Mediterranean, so it has become important for the consumer to be able to tell something of the characteristics of the oil from the bottle's label.

My favourite oils are thick and viscous, staying on salad rather than running straight off the leaves onto the plate, and peppery in their aftertaste. However, such an oil would be totally unsuitable for a mayonnaise, as would one heavily scented with the fragrance of melons or grass. For this reason the European Community has been working with a team of experts to establish a language for olive oil tasting, in the same way that words such as oaky are now widely accepted when used to describe wines. Some of the most interesting lectures that I have attended recently have been tutored olive oil tastings, and frequently the Italian oils are judged the best.

Estate Bottled Treasures

Hidden away throughout Italy are small estates producing exquisite oils in small quantities and often at high prices, the chateau bottled vintages of the olive oil world. Care must always be taken in the selection of oils as there are good and bad examples in every price range. A fancy bottle and label do not always indicate the best quality. Always use the best quality oil that you can afford, using it for salads as well as for cooking. Flavour is always an important consideration and, while you may feel you can use a slightly cheaper oil for basic cooking, the flavour of the oil will be very obvious in breads and in dishes where it is added as a last minute dressing or garnish.

Tips for Buying and Storing Olive Oil

The olive harvest takes place in the late summer or early autumn so the new season's oils are available from October onwards – the best shopkeepers outside Italy with the most rapid turnover of stock should be selling the new oils before Christmas.

Olive oil is not like a fine wine in as much as it does not improve with storage – it should really be used as young as possible. For this reason it is hoped that a labelling law will be introduced to state when the oil was produced. Olive oil is sensitive to air, light and heat. I buy my oil in gallon cans but the purists would say that this is not a good idea as air will enter the can as oil is dispensed, leading to a deterioration in quality by the end of the can. However, even with just two of us in the house, we do seem to get through a can in a matter of weeks. The best guidelines to follow are to store the oil in the dark, in a cool cupboard or larder. Once opened, the oil should be used in four to six weeks to enjoy it at its very best. Reseal an opened bottle as tightly as possible and always check any old oils by sniffing them before use – olive oil will become rancid when it is past its best.

Dressed and Stuffed for Cocktails

Of course olives are also very popular as antipasti, or for serving with drinks. Green olives tend to have a slightly sharper flavour than black, by virtue of the fact that they are picked and pickled when less mature. However, it is the green olives that are usually stuffed for cocktails. Once the pits or stones are removed the fruits may be stuffed with pimentos, almonds or anchovies, the latter being my favourite. I hope that this is all done by machine as I can think of little that can be less inspiring than stuffing olives for a living!

When buying olives, unless they are already packed in olive oil, I would suggest that you rinse them well under running water, to remove any brine solution which might make the olives taste slightly bitter. I then like to marinate the fruits to bring out their flavour. To create a delicious Italian flavour I use garlic, oregano, red chillis and plenty of flat-leaved parsley. I occasionally add just a few fillets of anchovy or three or four halves of sun-dried tomatoes, the latest food sensation from Italy.

Tomatoes – One of Italy's Most Famous Exports

Pomodoro, or 'golden apples' are as much a part of Italy as sunshine, olive oil and salami. Nothing can compare with the flavour of a tomato completely ripened in the Mediterranean sun! I have done a great deal of work for an Italian agricultural co-operative who produce many of the tomato products sold in our major supermarkets and I approached the first project with a great deal of trepidation – how was I going to find the enthusiasm to rave about canned tomatoes? (Being a fan of hairy men I had long subscribed to the theory that a kiss without a moustache is like a tomato without salt – tasteless!) However, the chopped Italian tomatoes so readily available today are the very best of produce, ripened in the sun and packed at the height of their flavour, producing a thick tomato sauce during processing rather than a thin watery juice. Such is their flavour that I would much rather use a can of Italian tomatoes than the glasshouse fruits, picked green and left to ripen in a cold store.

Tomatoes are grown throughout Italy and are a dominant ingredient in classic dishes from many regions. A few 'branches' of tomatoes are frequently hung in a cool place to air-dry, until required, at the end of the summer, thus extending the fresh tomato season. However, there is one tomato product that has caused a sensation outside Italy, to the extent that one would be forgiven for thinking that they must be eaten or used throughout the country. In truth, they are a peasant food of the south, of the region of Calabria, right down in the boot of Italy. I am referring to the phenomenon which is the sun-dried tomato.

Sun-drying for Preservation

Towards the end of the tomato season in Calabria bunches of the fruit are tied together and hung up on walls to dry in the late summer sunshine. The moisture in the fruit evaporates completely, leaving just the shrivelled shells of the tomatoes, deep red in colour and incredibly intense in their flavour. This is country food at its best. The southern Italians always favour strong seasonings so this method of tomato preservation is ideal for their cuisine.

The tomatoes are usually stored dry by the farming communities but, since these tomatoes have been 'discovered' by the rest of Europe, they are more commonly available bottled in olive oil, especially in supermarkets. Such processing is undertaken in established food processing plants, whereas I have heard that many of the packing houses that might have dealt with the dry tomatoes did not meet the stringent hygiene standards demanded by the major supermarket chains.

When cooking with sun-dried tomatoes the best possible results will be achieved if the tomatoes are peeled before use, as the skins often become tough during drying. To peel the tomatoes, soak them in boiling water for about ten minutes, refresh them in cold water and then peel off the skin from the flower end – tomato skins always pull off more easily if you move towards the stalk.

Are sun-dried tomatoes part of the classic cuisine of Italy? Well, in a word, no! They are currently so popular that it is easy to think that they must be but, having asked several leading authorities on Italian cookery exactly what they use the tomatoes for, the invariable answer has been 'nothing'! They are a food of the south, a country ingredient preserved in the simplest way possible.

Having said that, I must confess that I love them!

Sausages – Ancient and Modern

The preserved pork sausages of Italy are known as salami. Indeed, all the names such as salami, saucissons and sausages come from the Latin word 'salsus', meaning salted. The histories of ancient Rome record the tradition of sausage making and the word *salame* (the singular of salami) is used colloquially today to refer to an idiot with 'less brains than a sack of potatoes'!

Salami and Hams – the Cold Meats of Italy

All salami are raw meat, usually pork. The flavour of each variety of sausage is partially determined by the proportion of meat to fat, the meatier salami are the sweetest. The white dust that is often found on the outer casing is bacterial and contributes to the flavour of the sausage, but many other flavourings and spices such as peppercorns, spices and nuts, especially pistachios, are also used. Strangely enough, garlic is seldom added as it has a tendency to deteriorate. My favourite varieties of salami are ventracini (a very hot chilli sausage) and one flavoured with fennel. The latter is quite difficult to find but, as it is so delicious, it is well worth seeking out.

Salami are air-dried at a constant temperature, during which time they lose up to a third of their original weight through the evaporation of the water content of the sausages. This is very important because the salami will only store well if the meat is perfectly dry. Uncut salami may be stored for a considerable time at a cool room temperature but, once cut, it should be kept in the chiller in a shop, or in the refrigerator at home. Do not buy from a cut salami that is not refrigerated, and never buy from a sausage which has had all the casing removed from the meat – the salami will become dry and tough without the protective coating. Keep the salami well wrapped in the refrigerator to prevent drying.

Parma ham is the most famous of Italian hams and is air-dried in the same way as salami. It should really be referred to as *prosciutto crudo* – raw ham. Prosciutto is actually the Italian word for ham and may be applied to inferior products as well as to those of the Parma region – authentic quality hams will have a brand stamp on the skin of the ham, and will always come from the area around Parma.

The hams are rubbed with a mixture of sea salt and other spices, a process that is repeated twice before the hams are left to dry. The drying may take anything from 8 to 24 months, according to the size of the ham. They are then rubbed with very fine black pepper, which is clearly visible on the back of ham, where the meat is not covered with a thick layer of fat.

I would never recommend that you bring a souvenir of a whole ham back from your Italian holidays – if it seems like a bargain it is probably not a quality product, and it needs to be used quite quickly if it is to remain in good condition.

Prosciutto crudo may be frozen but will only keep for a comparatively short time – three months maximum – as the fat will start to become rancid. If you are trying to slice a ham at home you will need an extremely sharp knife. Cut away the thick layer of fat from the portion of meat that you are going to slice, and cut the meat very, very thinly, always allowing the knife to travel away from you – it is very easy for the knife to slip. The ham is actually easier to cut when it is tempered, or very lightly frozen. Wrap the cut surface of the ham tightly in foil or plastic film and store it in the refrigerator.

If you have a friendly local delicatessen I would strongly recommend that you make a bid for the knuckle of their next prosciutto crudo. The slices are usually too expensive to cook with, but the knuckle will impart the most wonderful flavour to pasta sauces and rich casseroles.

Fifty Cheeses to Choose From

Italy actually produces around 50 varieties of cheese. The best known, Parmesan, is made in the north, in the area around Parma also famed for its hams. For many years people outside Italy were content to dredge cheese from small cardboard tubs all over their pasta but this bears absolutely no resemblance to freshly grated Parmesan, which should always be used in preference. All supermarkets now stock blocks of Parmesan and they will keep for several weeks in the refrigerator if properly wrapped. It is one food that is definitely worth bringing home from your holidays! Good Parmesan is not sold under two years old (which accounts for its high price) and it will certainly keep if tightly wrapped in foil in the refrigerator. Parmesan is not, however, simply for scattering over cooked dishes; it is also very popular as a table cheese, either as a cheese course or as part of a selection of antipasti. It can also be used as a garnish for numerous savoury dishes by scraping curls of it from a block, either with a special tool or with a potato peeler. Never buy Parmesan unless it is labelled *Parmigiano Reggiano*, which should also be stamped on the rind – cheeses not bearing this mark may well be inferior.

There is not space here to discuss all the delicious Italian cheeses in detail, but they are splendid – in taste, texture and variety. Gorgonzola and dolcelatte (sweet milk) have long been popular blue cheeses – the former has a slightly sour flavour and is a better blue cheese for cooking; I love it melted into creamed polenta and served as a starter! Taleggio, a washed rind cheese similar to a Chaumes or Pont l'Eveque from France, is delicious when soft and was very popular in my delicatessen. Pecorino, which is a *grana* or hard cheese like Parmesan, is actually made from ewe's milk and has a slightly sharper flavour than Parmesan. I think that many dishes and sauces, especially pesto, are best made with a mixture of both Pecorino and Parmesan.

Two other Italian cheeses that must be mentioned are Ricotta and Mozzarella, both of which are now available in most supermarkets and which have really opened the door to authentic Italian cookery outside Italy. Ricotta is a soft cheese of similar fat content to a cottage cheese but with a smooth texture, making it a versatile ingredient for both sweet and savoury dishes. It mixes well with herbs and seasonings if you wish to eat it in salads but I really prefer it cooked, or in cheese-cake style desserts. It is frequently used to stuff tortellini and other pasta parcels.

Mozzarella is the traditional cheese for topping pizzas – it melts and becomes stringy and is easily recognised by its pure white colour. Originally made from buffalo's milk it is now more usually made from cow's milk and has a very slightly sour flavour. It really does melt well – I often top a snack such as a tomato bruschetta with thin slices of Mozzarella and pop it under a very hot grill until it melts. Mozzarella is also delicious in salads – not really for its own flavour but because it makes a wonderful combination with tomatoes, freshly chopped oregano or marjoram and lots of fruity green olive oil.

Emilia-Romagna – a Gourmet's Delight

In compiling the introduction to this book I felt that it was more important to deal with the foods of Italy that would not be covered elsewhere, than to discuss the regions of this fascinating country in any great detail. However, I cannot go on without introducing you, albeit briefly, to Emilia-Romagna.

This is *the* food area of Italy – it is certainly where I have eaten my most memorable Italian meals! The principal town is Bologna which everyone who has ever eaten spaghetti with a traditional meat sauce must have heard of – the town is deeply etched in the nation's culinary history! Just north of Bologna is Modena, the home of Ferrari and a town beloved of gourmets as the centre for balsamic vinegar. This is made from grape must, a new wine not properly fermented for drinking, and then aged in wooden barrels. It is mild but distinctive in flavour and is often added to sauces for meat and fish, as well as being used for dressings. Balsamic vinegar has only become popular outside Italy in the last decade, however, in the early seventeenth century, it was often the first article to be bequeathed in the wills of the people of this area. The town of Parma, so famed for its cheese and ham, lies a little further north; Ferrara, a town renowned for its baking, is to the east and Comacchio lies beside a huge lagoon where eels are farmed and many thousand fishermen make their living from the lake. The whole area is full of vineyards producing the grapes for lambrusco. I hope the shopping is as good in heaven as it is here!

A Peach of a Place

It has been impossible in these few pages to do justice to all the marvellous produce of Italy. As I write this it is summer and I have just enjoyed an Italian peach from the supermarket – even after travelling in a cold store across Europe I am convinced that the Italian peaches are the best and I would suggest that you always try to find them when you require canned or bottled peaches out of season.

On a trip to Emilia-Romagna I visited a fruit processing plant and was intrigued by the miraculously gentle yet so efficient machine that twisted the ripe peaches open and removed the stones – one quick twist and that was that; it's never so easy for me in the kitchen! The Italians actually prefer to buy their processed fruits in glass jars rather than in cans – it certainly enables you to see the extremely high quality of the fruit. Such fruits are worth seeking out for special occasions but the cost of transporting them in the glass is high, so you are more likely to find this quality Italian produce in Italian grocers or luxury stores outside Italy.

The following pages contain a mouth-watering selection of recipes – I hope they will inspire you as much as they have me. I have no doubt at all that the Italians have collected a great tradition of classic cooking throughout their colourful and eventful history. The Ancient Romans gave us so much – and the modern Italians continue to do so. Enjoy it!

SOUPS & STARTERS

Soups with Bits in!

The most striking thing about Italian soups is that they all have bits in them! There are no classic soups that are puréed or sieved after cooking, prior to being enriched with plenty of cream, to give a velvety smooth concoction. Some beans in soups may almost cook down to a purée but it is always possible to determine the main ingredient simply by looking! How my husband would have survived being brought up in an Italian household is beyond me as he would never touch a soup with 'bits in' when he was a small boy – luckily his attitude has now changed!

Italian soups are usually vegetable, fish or bean-based. Some fish soups are almost stews, substantial meals in themselves to be served only with fresh olive oil bread. Other soups, such as minestrone, may be thick or thin, the amount of vegetables and pasta, beans or potatoes used determining the final thickness and corporeity of the dish. Bean soups are the most warming and comforting for cold winter's days – I often make a soup of canned borlotti beans, onions, tomatoes and Italian herbs for a quick, warming lunch dish in the middle of winter.

There are, of course, exceptions that prove the rule. One soup very popular in the area around Rome is stracciatella, which literally means 'little rags' and contains no vegetables, fish or beans! It is a thin soup flavoured with Parmesan and has raw egg added to the boiling liquid which sets in strands or rags within the soup. It is comparatively light and an excellent soup for eating *al fresco* on a summer's evening.

Different regions of Italy are famed for specific soups – in the tomato growing areas of the south many of the soups (and other dishes) are based on tomatoes and their inseparable companions garlic and olive oil. At the opposite end of the country, in the north, where many green vegetables are grown, the soups reflect the local harvest, and in the central regions bean soups are the most popular.

Antipasti – the Ultimate Starter

Italian starters are my idea of heaven. In most countries just one starter is served, but the Italians often make a selection of tempting dishes and serve tiny quantities of each with a mixture of salami, cured meats and fish. The collective name for such dishes is antipasti. My idea of a heavenly weekend lunch is a selection of antipasti served with freshly baked foccacia, a delicious olive oil bread, and a bottle of wine. I lack the self-control to be able to enjoy antipasti as a starter to a large meal – I simply am not satisfied with just a very little of each dish!

The main advantage of serving antipasti for the busy cook is that very few of the dishes require any great preparation. In fact, you could serve a large selection of foods that have required no more from you than to be put onto plates! Rolls of salami, air-dried hams, tuna, sardines and a selection of olives may be complemented and augmented by dressed artichoke hearts, marinated mushrooms, hard boiled eggs and radishes. If you have time, add a cold caponata – an aubergine salad. Gourmet Mushrooms will turn an informal, family meal into a feast fit for the smartest of guests, prepared with the minimum of fuss. Of course, the success of such a meal is not down to just the sunshine – you do need to be prepared to spend time shopping for the very best ingredients to make your antipasti as flavoursome and memorable as possible. Many salads which are suitable for incorporating into a dish of mixed antipasti will be found in the later chapter on vegetables and salads.

Hot starters are more likely to stand alone as part of an Italian meal, more in the traditional style of an hors d'oeuvres. These need not be formal and may also be a relaxed way of chatting to friends over a leisurely first course. The hot garlic and anchovy dip bagna cauda makes a sociable starter, with plenty of crisp raw vegetables for dipping into the pot.

An International Favourite

Of course, one of the most famous of all Italian starters is ripe pieces of juicy melon wrapped in wafer thin slices of Parma ham or prosciutto crudo. More unusual is carpaccio, thin slices of raw beef flavoured with fresh herbs and olive oil, but this must be purchased, prepared and eaten on the same day as the beef is not preserved or treated in any way.

MILANESE VEGETABLE SOUP

A typically Italian vegetable soup - I sometimes add a little grated lemon rind for extra flavour.

Serves 4

INGREDIENTS
1 litre/1¾ pints chicken stock
1 chard leaf
½ carrot
½ aubergine
½ courgette
1 onion
1 stick celery
2 rashers smoked bacon
Salt and freshly ground black
  pepper
10 basil leaves

If using freshly made stock, carefully filter it through a fine muslin and then pour it into a saucepan and bring to the boil.

Cut all the vegetables (not the basil) and the bacon into small cubes, add to the stock and simmer gently for 15 minutes. Check the seasoning and add salt and pepper as necessary. Cut the basil leaves into thin strips and add them to the soup just before serving.

MINESTRONE

*Another variation on Italy's most famous soup! This variety
contains potatoes in place of pasta, making it suitable to
serve before a pasta main course.*

Serves 8-10

INGREDIENTS

225g/8oz dried white cannellini
  beans
2 tbsps olive oil
1 large ham bone, or prosciutto
  knuckle
1 onion, chopped
2 cloves garlic, crushed
4 sticks celery, sliced
2 carrots, diced
1 small head Savoy cabbage or
  460g/1lb fresh spinach, well
  washed
120g/4oz French beans, cut into
  2.5cm/1 inch lengths
225g/8oz tomatoes, peeled,
  seeded and diced
1 dried red chilli
2.8 litres/5 pints water (or half
  beef stock and water)
Salt and freshly ground black
  pepper
1 sprig fresh rosemary
1 bay leaf
3 potatoes, peeled and cut into
  small dice
3 courgettes, trimmed and cut
  into small dice
1 tbsp freshly chopped basil
1 tbsp freshly chopped parsley
Grated Parmesan cheese

Place the beans in a large bowl,
cover with cold water and leave
to soak overnight. Heat the oil in
a large stock pot and add ham
bone, onion and garlic. Cook
until the onion has softened but
not coloured. Add the celery,
carrots, cabbage and green
beans. If using spinach, reserve
until later. Drain and rinse the
beans and add them to the pot
with the tomatoes and the chilli
pepper. Add the water and bring
to the boil, skimming any fat
from the surface as necessary.
Add the rosemary and bay leaf
and simmer, uncovered, until the
beans are tender, about 1¼
hours.

 Add the potatoes and cook for a
further 20 minutes. Add the
courgettes and shredded spinach
and cook, skimming the surface
occasionally, for a further 15
minutes. Remove the ham bone,
rosemary and bay leaf and add
the basil and parsley. Season to
taste and serve with Parmesan
cheese.

MELON AND PROSCIUTTO

An incredibly popular starter in Italy and just about everywhere else! The success of this dish depends on the ripeness of the melon.

Serves 4

INGREDIENTS
1 large ripe melon
16 thin slices prosciutto ham

Cut the melon in half lengthways, scoop out the seeds and discard them. Cut the melon into quarters and carefully pare off the rind. Cut each quarter into four slices. Wrap each slice of melon in a slice of prosciutto and place on a serving dish. Alternatively, place the melon slices on the dish and cover with the slices of prosciutto, leaving the ends of the melon showing. Serve immediately.

BRUSCHETTA WITH TOMATOES

This is one of my favourite lunch-time snacks when tomatoes are ripe and full of flavour. Traditionally a starter, this is so delicious that I eat it at every opportunity! I sometimes smother the bread with tomatoes, if it is a snack, not a starter.

Serves 6-8

INGREDIENTS

18 slices of crusty Italian bread, cut 2.5cm/1 inch thick
2 cloves garlic, crushed
150ml/¼ pint olive oil
Salt and freshly ground black pepper
18 large fresh basil leaves
4-5 ripe tomatoes, depending on size

Preheat the oven to 190°C/375°F/Gas Mark 5. Place the sliced bread on a baking sheet and toast for about 10 minutes in the oven on each side. Spread some of the garlic on both sides of each slice. Heat the oil gently in a small saucepan. Arrange the bread on a serving plate and immediately drizzle with the warm oil. Sprinkle with salt and pepper. Slice the tomatoes in 1.25cm/½ inch rounds. Place one basil leaf and one slice of tomato on each slice of bread and serve immediately.

28

THYME SORBET

An unusual, but typically Italian sorbet used to cleanse the palate between fish and meat courses. Use any culinary thyme variety in flower.

Serves 4

INGREDIENTS
520ml/18 fl oz water
150g/5oz sugar
4 small sprigs fresh thyme in
  flower

Boil the water and sugar until a reasonably thick syrup is reached – this will take about 15 minutes. Remove from the heat and add the sprigs of thyme. Remove the thyme from the syrup after 2 minutes and drain the syrup through a very fine sieve. Pour into an ice cream maker and freeze. When the sorbet has crystallized, spoon into a container and keep in the freezer until needed. Alternatively, pour the strained syrup into a shallow container and place in the freezer until partly frozen. Remove from the freezer, gently break the mixture up with a fork, then return to the freezer until needed.

CARPACCIO WITH HERBS

Carpaccio is raw beef so it is essential to use top quality fresh meat for this recipe, and to shop, prepare and eat the beef on the same day. Carpaccio is an excellent starter for a summer dinner party.

Serves 4

INGREDIENTS
460g/1lb fresh fillet steak
4 basil leaves
5 chives
½ tsp freshly chopped coriander
3 mint leaves
½ tsp freshly chopped parsley
2 tbsps olive oil
Squeeze lemon juice
Salt and freshly ground black
    pepper
1 onion, cut into very thin slices

Slice the meat thinly and arrange it on a serving plate. Chop all the herbs together as finely as possible and stir them into the olive oil. Add a squeeze of lemon juice and some salt and pepper to the oil and herb mixture, then brush the sauce all over the slices of beef. Top with the sliced onion and serve.

SICILIAN CAPONATA

This dish of mixed vegetables may be served as an antipasta – a starter, or as a vegetable course. Choose a firm, shiny skinned aubergine – those that are wrinkled are generally bitter.

Serves 6

INGREDIENTS
1 aubergine
Salt
150ml/¼ pint olive oil
1 onion, sliced
2 red peppers, cored, seeded and cut into 2.5cm/1 inch pieces
2 sticks celery, sliced thickly
460g/1lb canned plum tomatoes
2 tbsps red wine vinegar
1 tbsp sugar
1 clove garlic, crushed
12 black olives, pitted
1 tbsp capers
Salt and freshly ground black pepper

Cut the aubergine in half and score the cut surface. Sprinkle with salt and leave to drain in a colander or on absorbent kitchen paper for 30 minutes. Rinse, pat dry and cut into 2.5cm/1 inch cubes. Heat the oil in a large frying pan and add the onion, peppers and celery. Lower the heat and cook for about 5 minutes, stirring occasionally. Add the aubergine and cook a further 5 minutes. Sieve the tomatoes to remove the seeds and add the pulp and liquid to the vegetables in the pan. Add the remaining ingredients except the olives and capers and cook for a further 2 minutes.

To remove the stones from the olives, roll them on a flat surface to loosen the stones and then remove them with a swivel vegetable peeler. Alternatively, use a cherry stoner. Cut the olives in quarters and add to the vegetables with the capers. Simmer, uncovered, over a moderate heat for 15 minutes to evaporate most of the liquid. Adjust the seasoning and serve hot or cold.

STRACCIATELLA SOUP

This is a thin soup with seasoned threads of egg which form when the egg mixture is added to the boiling chicken stock. It is a light but satisfying summer soup.

Serves 4-6

Ingredients

2 eggs
2 tbsps grated Parmesan cheese
2 tbsps fresh white breadcrumbs
2 tbsps clarified butter
Nutmeg
Salt and freshly ground black pepper
1.14 litres/2 pints chicken stock
2 tbsps freshly chopped parsley

Mix together the eggs, cheese, breadcrumbs, clarified butter and nutmeg. Season with salt and pepper and stir in 150ml/¼pint of chicken stock. Bring the remaining stock to the boil, then pour in the egg mixture, all at once. Whisk vigorously with a fork. Add the parsley and bring to the boil again. Serve at once.

GOURMET MUSHROOMS

The Italians are very fond of vegetable dishes, dressed in oil or mayonnaise, that can be served as antipasti – part of a mixed platter of meats and salads to start a meal. These Gourmet Mushrooms make excellent antipasti, served with a small selection of salami.

Serves 4

INGREDIENTS
340g/12oz button mushrooms
3 artichoke hearts, sliced thinly
Juice of 1 lemon
1 white celery heart, cut into fine
  strips
225g/8oz shrimps, cooked,
  shelled and de-veined
16 asparagus tips, cooked and
  drained
150ml/¼ pint mayonnaise
2 tbsps olive oil
2 ripe tomatoes, peeled and
  pressed through a sieve
Salt

Simmer the mushrooms for 15 minutes in a saucepan of water – use just enough water to cover the mushrooms. Drain them well. Sprinkle the artichoke hearts with half the lemon juice to keep them from darkening. Place the mushrooms, topped with artichokes, celery, shrimps and asparagus in little piles, in a large glass bowl. Chill.

Mix the mayonnaise with the oil, remaining lemon juice and the tomato pulp. Add salt to taste. Serve the sauce with the chilled vegetables.

BAGNA CAUDA – HOT VEGETABLE DIP

This is a simple country dish, a sociable way to start a meal with everyone dipping into the hot sauce. Cardoons, a vegetable popular in Italy and southern France, is almost a cross between celery, fennel and Jerusalem artichokes.

Serves 4

INGREDIENTS
3 cloves garlic
225ml/8 fl oz olive oil
60g/2oz can anchovies in oil, chopped

Cut the garlic cloves into very thin strips and cook them in the oil until soft. Keep the garlic from browning and consequently losing its flavour. Remove the pan from the heat and add the anchovies. Crush the anchovies with a wooden spoon. Replace the pan on the heat and keep the dip hot.

This "bagna cauda," as it is known in Piedmontese dialect, is served in the pan in which it is made, which should ideally be a glazed earthenware bowl, called a "fojot", which is kept hot either with coals or over a very low chafing-dish flame. The bagna cauda is placed in the centre of the table and each person dips strips of raw or very lightly cooked vegetables into it. The classic vegetable used by the Piedmontese is the cardoon, but you may use any of the following: green peppers, raw, lightly parboiled or in oil; or, celery, cabbage, Jerusalem artichoke, potatoes, etc, raw or lightly cooked, as appropriate.

A refinement of bagna cauda calls for adding, just before using, a few tablespoons of double cream and a thinly sliced white truffle.

MINESTRONE ALLA MILANESE

Minestrone is probably the Italian national soup, and there are many different recipes for it. This recipe, for a Milanese minestrone, is thickened with rice rather than pasta, and contains borlotti beans rather than haricots.

Serves 6

INGREDIENTS
4 rashers of bacon
120g/4oz bacon rind
1 bunch parsley, chopped
1 clove garlic, chopped
1 stalk celery, chopped
2 potatoes, chopped
2 carrots, chopped
1 courgette, chopped
120g/4oz green beans, cut into short lengths
120g/4oz dried borlotti beans or navy beans, soaked overnight and drained
3 tomatoes, peeled and diced
Salt
120g/4oz Savoy cabbage, finely shredded
225g/8oz rice

Chop the bacon extremely finely until it is almost a pulp. Place the bacon, bacon rind, parsley, garlic, and celery in a large saucepan and cook for 5 minutes. Add the potatoes, carrots, courgette, green beans, dried beans and tomatoes. Cover with water and season with salt. Bring to the boil over a high heat, then lower the heat and simmer, covered, for at least 2 hours. Add water from time to time to keep up the level of the liquid.

After the first hour, add the cabbage. Thirty minutes before serving, add the rice and simmer, being careful to keep the rice 'al dente' and not to allow it to become soft and mushy. Remove the bacon rind and season the soup to taste with salt. Serve with a little grated Parmesan cheese, if liked.

PAPPA AL POMODORO - BREAD AND TOMATO SOUP

This is a simple soup of basic Italian ingredients: bread, tomatoes, garlic and basil. The olive oil is an extra seasoning, added just before serving.

Serves 4-5

INGREDIENTS

225g/8oz firm white bread, crusts removed
460g/1lb tomatoes
1.14 litres/2 pints chicken broth
2 cloves garlic, chopped
2 tbsps freshly chopped basil
Salt and freshly ground black pepper
Olive oil for serving

Roughly chop the bread and soak it in water for 30 minutes Drain and squeeze the bread very thoroughly. Peel the tomatoes, remove the seeds and chop the flesh finely.

Bring the stock to the boil in a large saucepan. Stir in the bread, the chopped tomatoes, garlic and basil. Season with salt and pepper. Cook, covered, for 10-15 minutes. Hand the olive oil round separately when serving, allowing each person to mix a little into the hot soup.

DONZELLINE RIPIENE DI ACCUIGHE - ANCHOVY PUFFS

These puffs make wonderful cocktail party savouries. The dough is rather like a scone mixture and cooks very quickly.

Serves 6

INGREDIENTS
120g/4oz butter
150g/5oz plain flour
Milk
60g/2oz can anchovy fillets,
    chopped
Olive oil

Cut the butter into the flour until the particles are very fine. Stir in enough milk to make a stiff dough. Knead on a floured surface until smooth, then cover and chill for 30 minutes.

Divide into two equal parts. Roll both out thinly. Scatter the anchovies over one piece of dough, and cover with the remaining piece. Roll out again, as thinly as possible, and cut into small triangles, discarding any pieces without anchovy. Heat a little olive oil in a large frying pan and fry the 'puffs' quickly till golden on both sides. Add more oil when necessary. Drain on absorbent kitchen paper and serve hot.

LIVORNESE FISH SOUP

This fish soup is spiced with chilli and garlic, making it a perfect choice for entertaining on bright but cool autumn evenings. I love fish soups!

Serves 4

INGREDIENTS

1.6kg/3½lbs mixed fish (including small whole fish such as sprats and a little shellfish but no smoked fish)
3 tbsps olive oil
1 carrot, sliced
1 onion, sliced
1 small chilli, seeded and chopped
Small bunch parsley, well rinsed and dried
120ml/4 fl oz white wine
3 cloves garlic
4 tomatoes, quartered
Salt and freshly ground black pepper
1 loaf Italian ciabata bread
60g/2oz finely grated Parmesan cheese

Clean, gut and rinse the fish and shellfish, skin any fillets and cut them into large pieces. Heat the olive oil in a large pan and gently fry the carrots, onion, chilli and the parsley. Add the fish and shellfish and continue frying for 4 minutes.

Add the dry white wine and cook until almost evaporated, then stir in the garlic and the tomatoes. Continue cooking for a few minutes, then add plenty of water. Bring to the boil, reduce the heat, and simmer gently for 1 hour. Taste the soup and adjust the seasoning as necessary.

Cut the ciabata into slices and toast them under the grill.

Strain the soup through a fine sieve, pressing the fish well to extract all the flavour. Serve the soup piping hot, spooned over the toast and sprinkled with the grated Parmesan cheese.

WHITE BEAN AND TUNA FISH SALAD

Tonno e fagioli is a favourite Tuscan dish. It may be served as a main course salad but I prefer to use it as part of a selection of antipasti, as a starter or a lazy weekend main course.

Serves 4

INGREDIENTS
430g/15oz can haricot or
   cannellini beans, drained
200g/7oz can tuna fish, drained
   and flaked
3 tbsps olive oil
1 tbsp lemon juice
1 tsp white wine vinegar
1 tsp Dijon mustard
1 clove garlic, crushed
Salt and freshly ground black
   pepper
1 small onion, finely sliced
Black olives to taste
1 tbsp freshly chopped parsley

Mix the beans and flaked tuna together in a serving dish.

Combine the oil, lemon juice, wine vinegar, mustard, garlic, salt and pepper to make a dressing and pour it over the beans and tuna. Add the sliced raw onion, the black olives and chopped parsley, and serve.

VEGETABLES & SALADS

Vegetables and salads play an important part in an Italian meal as the country produces such an enormous wealth and variety of fruits and vegetables. Individual vegetables are celebrated in salads, many of which are suitable for serving as starters, as part of a mixed selection of antipasti. The Italians find exquisite and inventive ways of preparing and cooking vegetables, to serve either with meat and fish, or as a separate course, in much the same way as in France.

Tomatoes, onions, aubergines, courgettes, mushrooms, white truffles, peas and broccoli – none of these vegetables are rare; indeed, all are very well known throughout Europe (with the possible exception of the truffles). However, the Mediterranean climate allows the vegetables to ripen naturally in the sun and this, I firmly believe, allows the natural flavours of the produce to be developed to their limits, so that the vegetables are bursting with brightness and immediacy. Yes, we can obtain all these vegetables in our cosmopolitan modern supermarkets, but even Italian vegetables picked for export cannot match the delights of those left to ripen in their native sunlight before being picked, cooked and served as quickly as possible.

Sun-ripened Sweetness

Tomatoes (yes, I know they are really a fruit!) are a case in point. Most tomato products – purées, pastes and concentrates – that are widely available in supermarkets and grocer's shops are Italian in origin. Fresh tomatoes eaten in Italy are juicy and bursting with flavour. Pick them, even the plum tomatoes, when slightly under-ripe and export them, allowing the produce to ripen slowly in transit, and the immediacy and excitement of flavour is lost. I would rather use a can of Italian tomatoes, preserved when at the height of their ripeness and thus packed with all their flavour, than an under-ripe, greenhouse tomato which has never seen the sun! Passata, a pulp of crushed and sieved tomatoes, is another excellent Italian product for use in the kitchen, producing the most delicious soup bases, stews and sauces.

Perfect Artichokes

The Italians, like the French, grow huge quantities of globe artichokes. Try just the hearts sautéed in typical Italian style with the classic seasonings of parsley, garlic and freshly ground black pepper – delicious! The artichokes are, however, most commonly served preserved in vinaigrette. A word of warning – beware of those tempting jars on supermarket and delicatessen shelves containing artichoke antipasti – more often than not the artichokes are tough and papery. If you find a brand that is good, then stick to it. I have taken to buying canned artichoke hearts (which are nigh-on tasteless by themselves) and enlivening them with a home-made dressing, which gives a much more palatable result.

A Little Ham for Flavour

Italian white onions are mild in flavour and of a reasonable size for stuffing – three onions per person gives a good helping, looking more attractive and cooking a good deal more quickly than one large onion each. The Italians are famed for their hams and dried meats, and just a little will add significant flavour to a dish of vegetables. Small amounts of ham develop the flavour of the main ingredient and also make a vegetable dish a little more substantial. Included in this chapter are recipes for fennel and asparagus, both of which are cooked with ham. One of my favourite ways of cooking broccoli is to serve it with some crispy fried pancetta, a dry, flavoursome Italian bacon.

There are many delicious Italian salads but the success of these, as of any salad, will depend on the quality of the ingredients that you have to start with. Limp tired ingredients will be soft and unpalatable; under-ripe vegetables will be crunchy and lacking in flavour. One of the most famous of all salads is that of tomato, mozzarella and avocado, the colours of the ingredients representing those of the Italian flag. The only requirement for this salad is to have top quality ripe ingredients: made with ripe vegetables and fresh cheese the salad is sublime – made with under-ripe tomatoes and a hard avocado it is awful!

Most salads that are not already coated in olive oil require a dressing. I have included a recipe for an Italian salad dressing in this chapter but many people prefer to use just olive oil on their vegetables. This, of course, is up to you but I often find just oil alone a little too rich and prefer to use a dressing which includes a little vinegar.

SAUTÉED SLICED ARTICHOKE HEARTS WITH PARSLEY AND GARLIC

Warm artichokes with the classic Italian seasonings of garlic, parsley and olive oil – delicious!

Serves 4

INGREDIENTS
8 large artichokes
2 cloves garlic, chopped
7 tbsps olive oil
Salt and freshly ground black
  pepper
2 tbsps freshly chopped parsley

Remove all the artichoke leaves and trim off the hairy choke, leaving only the fleshy heart of the artichoke. Slice the artichoke hearts into strips. Sauté the garlic in the oil briefly, then add the artichoke strips and season with salt and pepper. Cook for several minutes over a high heat, then lower the heat and continue cooking until the artichoke strips are tender, about 30 minutes. Sprinkle freshly chopped parsley over the artichokes just before serving.

SAUTÉED BROCCOLI WITH GARLIC

A lovely way to serve broccoli – I sometimes add crispy shreds of pancetta, a dry Italian bacon.

Serves 4

INGREDIENTS

900g/2lbs broccoli, washed
60g/2oz butter
2 cloves garlic, chopped
2 tsps freshly chopped parsley
Salt and freshly ground black
  pepper

Cut the broccoli into florets and trim off the stalks. Cook all the parts of the broccoli in salted, boiling water for 5 minutes. Rinse in cold water to freshen, then set aside to drain.

Melt the butter in a frying pan, stir in the garlic and parsley and then add the broccoli florets. Fry for a few minutes. Season with plenty of salt and pepper and serve hot.

ROMAN-STYLE ARTICHOKES

In this recipe just the hearts of the artichokes are used. They are topped with a tomato and basil sauce and baked.

Serves 4

INGREDIENTS
Juice of 2 lemons
16 small artichokes
4 large tomatoes, peeled, seeded
    and roughly chopped
1 tbsp freshly chopped chives
2 tbsps olive oil
5 fresh basil leaves, chopped
Salt and freshly ground black
    pepper
4 tbsps grated Parmesan cheese

Preheat the oven to
200°C/400°F/Gas Mark 6.

Fill a bowl with water and add the lemon juice. Cut the hard stalks off the artichokes and, using a small, sharp knife, cut off all the leaves, leaving the hearts whole. Place the artichoke hearts in the bowl of lemon water as soon as the leaves are removed, to prevent discolouration. Cook the artichoke hearts in salted, boiling water for 15-20 minutes until tender.

Mix together the chives, tomato, 1 tbsp olive oil, basil and plenty of salt and pepper. Remove the hairy choke from each artichoke heart. Grease an ovenproof dish with the remaining oil and place the hearts in the dish. Spoon the tomato sauce over each heart, sprinkle with the Parmesan cheese and cook in the hot oven until crisp, about 10-15 minutes. Serve hot.

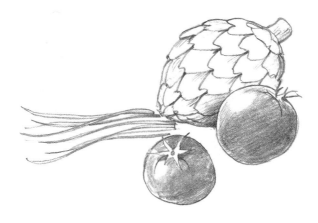

STUFFED WHITE ONIONS

White onions are mild in flavour and attractive in appearance. These are stuffed with a typical Italian mix of veal, parsley and Parmesan.

Serves 4

INGREDIENTS

12 white Italian onions, peeled
225g/8oz veal
1 tbsp freshly chopped parsley
1 tsp Madeira
1 tbsp olive oil
Salt and freshly ground black
  pepper
2 tbsps grated Parmesan cheese

Preheat the oven to 200°C/400°F/Gas Mark 6. Cook the peeled onions in lightly salted, boiling water for 10 minutes. Drain well. Hollow out the centre of each onion, reserving the scooped out onion flesh.

Finely chop the reserved onion flesh. Chop the meat in a food processor and then stir in the chopped onion, parsley, Madeira and 1 tsp of olive oil. Season with salt and pepper. Fill each hollowed-out onion with the veal mixture.

Grease an ovenproof dish with the remaining olive oil and place the onions in the dish. Cook in the preheated oven for 15 minutes, then sprinkle the grated Parmesan cheese over each stuffed onion and serve.

POTATO CAKES

Olive oil and potatoes is a winning combination! These crispy potato cakes go well with any meat or fish dishes.

Serves 4

INGREDIENTS
4 large potatoes, peeled and finely grated
1 tbsp freshly chopped parsley
1 tbsp finely grated onion
Salt and freshly ground black pepper
4 tbsps olive oil

Mix together the potato, parsley and onion, then season with plenty of salt and pepper. Heat 1 tbsp olive oil in a non-stick frying pan. Place one quarter of the potato mixture in the frying pan and flatten out with the back of a spoon into a largish round. Cook over a gentle heat until crisp and golden on one side, then turn and cook on the other side. Repeat with the remaining mixture until you have 4 potato cakes. Keep the potato cakes warm in a low oven until required.

ROMANY AUBERGINES

*This gypsy-style recipe uses country ingredients for a
delicious, tangy dish. Serve hot, or cold as a salad.*

Serves 4

INGREDIENTS
2 large aubergines
1 thick rasher smoked bacon
1 slice ham
12 slices Parma ham
2 tbsps olive oil
30g/1oz butter
1 onion, chopped
1 shallot, chopped
½ tsp freshly chopped rosemary
3 tbsps crushed tomato pulp or
   passata
60ml/2 fl oz white wine
Salt and freshly ground black
   pepper

Cut the aubergines into slices.

Bring a large saucepan of lightly
salted water to the boil, then add
the slices of aubergine and cook
for 2 minutes. Remove the
aubergine slices with a slotted
spoon, drain and then set aside
on absorbent kitchen paper to
remove any excess water.

Cut the bacon, ham and Parma
ham into thin strips. Heat the oil
and the butter together in a large
frying pan and gently fry the
onion, shallot, rosemary, the
hams and the bacon together for
a few minutes. Stir in the tomato
pulp and the white wine, then
season with salt and pepper.
Spread the well-drained
aubergine slices over the tomato
sauce in the pan and cook,
covered, for 5 minutes. Remove
the cover and continue cooking
until the sauce has thickened and
the juices have almost
evaporated. Serve either hot or
cold.

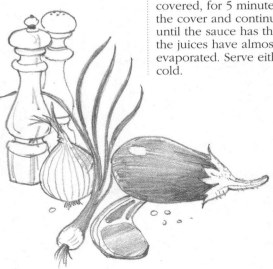

TOMATO SALAD RUSTICA

Sun-ripened tomatoes have an intensity of flavour that is unforgettable. Choose firm, ripe tomatoes for this dish – and remember that they were originally called 'Love Apples'!

Serves 4

INGREDIENTS
4-6 anchovies
Milk
460g/1lb tomatoes
1 onion
2 tbsps capers
1 tsp freshly chopped oregano or
    basil
Salt and freshly ground black
    pepper
90ml/3 fl oz olive oil
1 tbsp lemon juice

Soak the anchovies in a little milk before using – this removes any excess saltiness. Rinse, pat dry and chop the anchovies. Cut the tomatoes into quarters and remove the cores. Slice each quarter in half again and place them in a serving bowl. Slice the onion into rounds and then separate into rings. Scatter over the tomatoes. Add the anchovies to the tomatoes and onions along with the capers.

Mix the herbs, salt, pepper, oil and lemon juice together until well emulsified and pour the dressing over the salad. Mix all the ingredients gently and leave to stand for about 30 minutes before serving.

FRIED COURGETTES AND COURGETTE FLOWERS

Fried courgette flowers are very fashionable. Served in this way, with courgettes and a garlic and anchovy seasoning, they make a very sophisticated dish.

Serves 4

INGREDIENTS
½ clove garlic
6 anchovy fillets
200ml/7 fl oz warm water
120g/4oz flour, sifted
2 tbsps olive oil
Salt and freshly ground black pepper
2 egg whites
20 small courgettes with their flowers intact, carefully washed and patted dry with kitchen paper
Oil for deep-frying

Pound the garlic and anchovies together in a mortar until quite smooth, then add the warm water. Place the flour in a large mixing bowl and whisk in the flavoured water and then the olive oil. Season with salt and pepper. Stiffly beat the egg whites until they hold their shape, then fold them carefully into the batter.

Heat the oil to approximately 170°C/345°F. Dip the courgettes and their flowers, one by one, into the batter and then fry them quickly in the oil. Remove when crisp and golden, and set aside to drain on absorbent kitchen paper. Serve hot.

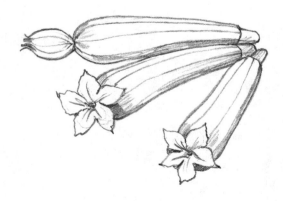

PEPPER SALAD WITH CAPERS

Capers are not pickled nasturtium seeds – they are the flower heads of a trailing plant that grows well in Italy and other Mediterranean countries. They are a popular summer seasoning.

Serves 4-6

INGREDIENTS

3 large peppers, red, green and yellow
90ml/3 fl oz olive oil
1 clove garlic, finely chopped
6-8 basil leaves, roughly chopped
1 tbsp freshly chopped marjoram
2 tbsps capers
1 tbsp white wine vinegar
Salt and freshly ground black pepper

Cut the peppers in half and remove the core and seeds. Press with the palm of the hand or the back of a knife to flatten. Brush the skin side with oil and place the peppers under a preheated grill. Grill the peppers until the skins are well charred. Wrap in a damp tea-towel and leave for 15 minutes. Unwrap and peel off the charred skin.

Cut the peppers into thick strips and arrange them on a serving dish. Scatter with the chopped garlic, basil, marjoram and capers. Mix the remaining olive oil with the vinegar and salt and pepper and pour over the salad. Refrigerate for 1 hour before serving.

STUFFED COURGETTE FLOWERS

*I always enjoy courgettes cooked with herbs and cream. This
wonderful dish uses the courgette flowers, stuffed with a
creamy fish filling – it is very sophisticated.*

Serves 4

INGREDIENTS
200g/7oz white fish fillets
3 tbsps freshly chopped chives
1 egg
280ml/½ pint single cream
Salt and freshly ground black
   pepper
1 tbsp double cream
12 courgette flowers, carefully
   washed and dried

Place the fish, 1 tbsp of the
freshly chopped chives, the egg
and 1 tbsp of the single cream in
a liquidiser or food processor.
Blend until smooth, then press
the fish mixture through a fine

sieve and season with salt and
pepper. Place in the refrigerator
for 30 minutes. Beat the double
cream into the fish stuffing and
place the stuffing in a piping bag
fitted with a large plain nozzle.

Gently ease open the petals of
the courgette flowers and fill the
centre with the stuffing. Reshape
the outer petals and set the
flowers to cook in a steamer for
approximately 12 minutes. Heat
the remaining single cream with
the remaining chives, season,
and serve the courgette flowers
with the sauce poured over.

SICILIAN RATATOUILLE

I love ratatouille and make it in a number of different ways at home. This recipe is typically Italian, flavoured with olives and capers – it is delicious hot or cold.

Serves 4

INGREDIENTS
1 aubergine, cut into small cubes
Oil for deep-frying
10 green olives, pitted
2 tbsps olive oil
½ stick celery, cut into small
  pieces
1 large onion, sliced
1 tsp capers
2-3 cloves garlic, chopped
1 tbsp freshly chopped parsley
3 large tomatoes, peeled, seeded
  and roughly chopped
Salt and freshly ground black
  pepper

Fry the aubergines in moderately hot oil, taking care that they do not brown. Remove with a slotted spoon and drain on absorbent kitchen paper. Cut the pitted olives into thin slices.

Heat the olive oil and cook the celery, onion, olives, capers, garlic and parsley together for 1 minute. Stir in the chopped tomato and fried aubergine and season with salt and pepper. Cook over a gentle heat for approximately 30 minutes. Stir gently, from time to time, to prevent sticking. Season to taste before serving.

AUBERGINES SCAPECE

This is a most unusual and delicious salad – fried aubergine slices spread with anchovy and garlic and marinated before serving.

Serves 4

INGREDIENTS

Oil for deep-frying
2 large, unblemished aubergines, sliced
4 anchovy fillets
1 tbsp freshly chopped parsley
½ tsp hot pepper sauce
1 clove garlic
Salt and freshly ground black pepper
120ml/4 fl oz sherry or wine vinegar

Heat the oil until moderately hot, then gently fry the aubergine slices. Do not allow them to brown. Set aside on absorbent kitchen paper to drain.

Crush together the anchovies, parsley, hot pepper sauce and garlic in a pestle and mortar. Season with salt and a little pepper, then stir in the vinegar.

Spread the aubergine slices out on a large serving plate and spoon the anchovy sauce over them. Marinate for 1½ hours and serve at room temperature.

WINTER SALAMI RISOTTO

*This is a rice salad flavoured with cold meats and vegetables
– just the sort of salad I love!*

Serves 4

INGREDIENTS
225g/8oz salami, thinly sliced
120-175g/4-6oz assorted Italian
  cured meats
2 green peppers
1 red pepper
4 large ripe tomatoes
90g/3oz green beans, cooked
8 stuffed olives
150g/5oz arborio rice, cooked
3-4 tbsps Italian dressing

Chop some of the meats and roll the remainder into little cigar shapes. Chop most of the vegetables, leaving a few large pieces for garnish. Slice the stuffed olives. Blend the rice with the dressing, chopped meat, chopped vegetables and olives and place in a salad bowl. Top with the larger pieces of vegetables and rolls of meat.

Serve with a green salad.

ASPARAGI IN FORNO ALL'ITALIANA – BAKED ASPARAGUS ITALIAN STYLE

It is too easy to just eat asparagus without any embellishment. As the season progresses I welcome fresh serving ideas and this recipe is particularly delicious.

Serves 4

INGREDIENTS
24 asparagus spears
4 thick slices prosciutto crudo, fat and lean, or ham
90g/3oz butter, melted
120g/4oz grated Parmesan
4 slices toast (made by frying bread in butter)
Salt

Preheat the oven to 200°C/400°F/Gas Mark 6. Clean the asparagus and trim any tough ends. Remove scales, and tie the asparagus in a bundle. Cook the asparagus standing upright with tips above boiling water. Use a suitable coffee pot for this. Drain while still al dente, untie the bundle and allow the asparagus to cool completely.

Wrap 6 asparagus tips in each slice of ham and arrange the rolls in a lightly buttered shallow baking dish. Pour about 2 tbsp of melted butter over them, sprinkle with grated Parmesan, then pour a little more melted butter over the Parmesan. Bake in the preheated oven until well browned, about 15 minutes. Meanwhile, brown the bread slices in the remaining butter and transfer them to a serving dish. Place the ham asparagus rolls on the toast and serve.

POMODORI CASALINGHI RIPIENI – COOK'S STUFFED TOMATOES

Use large sun-ripened tomatoes to achieve a real Italian flavour in this dish. Serve as a lunch or supper dish with salad and Italian olive oil bread. Do not overcook the tomatoes or they will collapse.

Serves 4

INGREDIENTS
8 tomatoes
Salt and freshly ground black
  pepper
1 small onion, chopped
120g/4oz butter
250g/9oz soft breadcrumbs
90g/3oz grated Parmesan
A few basil leaves, chopped
6 sprigs parsley, chopped
2 anchovy fillets
60g/2oz pine nuts, ground in a
  mortar

Preheat the oven to
180°C/350°F/Gas Mark 4. Cut a
thin slice off the tops of the
tomatoes. Scoop out the seeds,
then squeeze the tomato cups
lightly over a bowl to catch the
juice. Sprinkle the tomatoes
lightly with salt and invert them
on a rack set over a tin. Leave for
30 minutes. Reserve the juice.

Sauté the onion in 60g/2oz of the
butter until golden. Add the
breadcrumbs, grated Parmesan,
basil, parsley, anchovy fillets and
pine nuts. Sprinkle with salt and
pepper and stir in the reserved
tomato juice. Mix well.

Arrange the tomato cups side by
side in a buttered baking dish,
and stuff with the filling. Dot
with the remaining butter and
bake in the preheated oven for
20 minutes or until tomatoes are
tender but still hold their shape.

FINOCCHI AL BURRO CON PROSCIUTTO – BUTTERED FENNEL WITH HAM

Many people find fennel to be an acquired taste but it is very refreshing on a hot day. It has an aniseed flavour which blends well with the cheese.

Serves 4

INGREDIENTS
4 fennel roots ('finocchi')
60g/2oz butter
1 small onion, finely chopped
120g/4oz ham, chopped
430ml/¾ pint chicken stock
Salt
60g/2oz grated Parmesan

Discard the tough outer layers of the fennel, then cut the bulbs into wedges. Heat the butter and sauté the onion. Add the ham with the fennel and cook over a low heat for about 10 minutes. Add the stock and boil until the stock is evaporated. Season to taste with salt. Sprinkle the grated Parmesan over the fennel, remove from the heat and serve.

TOMATO, AVOCADO AND MOZZARELLA SALAD WITH BASIL

This is the most famous salad in Italy – red, white and green to match the colours of the national flag. Choose prime quality ingredients for maximum flavour.

Serves 4

INGREDIENTS
4 large tomatoes
400g/14oz Mozzarella
2 large avocados
Lemon juice
Olive oil
Salt and freshly ground black
  pepper
Fresh basil

Arrange slices of tomato, Mozzarella and avocado on individual plates. Dip the avocado in lemon juice to avoid discolouration. Drizzle the salad with a little olive oil, add some chopped basil, season the dish with plenty of freshly ground black pepper and a little salt.

Serve with plenty of crusty bread.

COURGETTE, CAPER AND ANCHOVY SALAD

The real secret of this salad is to slice the courgettes very thinly, either by hand or machine. They are then able to absorb much more of the delicious flavouring of anchovies and capers.

Serves 4

INGREDIENTS
460g/1lb courgettes
1 small onion, thinly sliced
1 tbsp capers
4-6 anchovies, chopped
1 tbsp anchovy oil (drained from the can of anchovies)
2 tbsps olive oil
2 tbsps tarragon vinegar
Juice of ½ lemon
Salt and freshly ground black pepper

Garnish
2 sprigs rosemary
2 whole anchovies

Trim the courgettes and slice them very thinly. Mix with the onion, capers and chopped anchovies. Mix the anchovy oil, olive oil, tarragon vinegar and lemon juice together, then add salt and pepper to taste. Stir the dressing into the prepared salad ingredients and garnish with anchovies and rosemary.

STUFFED MUSHROOMS

Try to get large field mushrooms for this dish – they have a
wonderful flavour. The mushroom stalks may be chopped
finely and added to the stuffing.

Serves 4

INGREDIENTS

4 tbsps butter or margarine,
  melted
4 cloves garlic, crushed
2 onions, finely chopped
½ tsp nutmeg
1 tbsp olive oil
4 large or 8 medium mushrooms,
  stalks removed
225g/8oz spinach, trimmed,
  cooked and finely chopped
2 tbsps fresh white breadcrumbs
Salt and freshly ground black
  pepper
1 egg, beaten

Garnish
1 tbsp freshly chopped parsley

Preheat the oven to
200°C/400°F/Gas Mark 6. Heat
the butter in a pan. Add the
garlic, onion and nutmeg and fry
gently until the onion has
softened. Remove from the pan
and set aside to cool.

Meanwhile, heat the oil in the
pan and sauté the mushrooms on
both sides until lightly browned.
Place upside-down in a shallow
ovenproof dish. Mix together the
onion mixture, spinach,
breadcrumbs and salt and freshly
ground black pepper to taste. Stir
in the beaten egg. Cover each
mushroom cap with the mixture,
shaping neatly. Cover with
aluminium foil and bake in the
hot oven for 10 minutes. Serve
immediately, garnished with
chopped parsley.

STUFFED RADICCHIO

Radicchio is not actually a lettuce, but the Italian name for all forms of chicory. It is most often, however, applied to the round, red variety used in salads. The fact that radicchio is of the chicory family explains its slightly bitter taste.

Serves 4

INGREDIENTS
200g/7oz can tuna fish, drained
60g/2oz rice, cooked
1 radicchio (8 good whole
  leaves; the rest finely chopped)
1 tbsp freshly chopped parsley
1 tsp lemon juice
2 tbsps capers
2 tbsps double cream, whipped
2 tbsps vermouth or dry sherry
Salt and freshly ground black
  pepper

Garnish
Lemon slices
Parsley

Flake the tuna fish and mix with the rice, chopped radicchio, parsley, lemon juice, capers, double cream, wine and salt and pepper to taste.

Divide the mixture evenly between 4 whole radicchio leaves and place the remaining 4 on top. Serve garnished with lemon slices and parsley.

ITALIAN SALAD DRESSING

This is a vinaigrette dressing with a difference. Balsamic vinegar, an Italian speciality, gives a sweetness and lightness to the dressing. I sometimes add crushed anchovy fillets, capers or a little garlic to the dressing for extra flavour.

Serves 4

INGREDIENTS

120ml/4 fl oz extra virgin olive oil
2 tbsps balsamic vinegar
1 tsp sugar
1 tbsp freshly chopped flat leaved parsley
Salt and freshly ground black pepper

Place all the ingredients in a screw-topped jar or a vinaigrette shaker and shake until well blended. The dressing may also be mixed in a shallow bowl with a small whisk. Taste the dressing, adjust the seasoning if necessary and use with vegetables and salads.

LIGHT LUNCHES & SUPPER DISHES

I don't think it's just me – I'm sure that most people really only want to eat one large meal a day. In keeping with many, my life-style dictates that, during the week, this should be in the evening. At the weekend, however, when there is more chance to relax and un-wind, I definitely favour a long leisurely lunch and a long leisurely snooze to follow! This chapter is not about recipes for such an idyllic way of life – it is for the former regime, when time is at a premium and only a light meal is required, either at midday or in the evening, after work. Plenty of dishes included in other chapters of this book, especially those for pizzas, crespelle and some pasta dishes, are also suitable for lunches and suppers, but this chapter includes some of my favourites.

A Warm Salad – a Complete Light Meal

I have included a number of warm salads in this chapter as I always feel that they are so much more satisfying than the cold varieties and make a simple, complete meal. The Goat's Cheese Salad with Tarragon and the Chicken Liver Salad are two of my favourite recipes. In Italy, as in so many countries, there are numerous local goat's cheeses, all with their own robust, individual characteristics, so it is impossible actually to suggest which cheese you should use for the salad. I recommend seeking out a cheese produced locally – there are good goat's cheese producers everywhere, at home and abroad. Failing that, most large supermarkets now stock two or three varieties of goat's cheese – choose one that is firm enough to keep its shape. Very fresh, soft goat's cheese has the consistency of runny cottage cheese and would not be suitable for this recipe. I sometimes use a mould ripened cheese – one that has a white rind, similar to that of a Brie.

I have found that because the Italians use so much pasta, polenta and rice, they cook only infrequently with pastry. When they do, however, the dishes are memorable. I have included a recipe for a wonderful Seafood Torta, a flan with a filling of white fish, prawns and crab bound together in a white wine sauce flavoured with hot pepper flakes, in the spicy tradition of southern Italy.

A Tasty Squid Salad

Some of my favourite Italian dishes are based on squid – the only trouble is that I tend to eat so much of them that I am less than enthusiastic about any other parts of a meal that might follow! For that reason I particularly enjoy recipes such as the Chick Pea Salad which includes squid and may be enjoyed as a meal in itself – perfect for a light lunch or supper dish.

Chicken livers are economical, versatile and quick to cook. Even a combination of such simple ingredients as livers, some peas, butter and parsley can produce a deliciously nutritious supper dish. Serve over wholemeal toast if you wish, but I find one of the lighter Italian olive oil breads allows the flavours of the livers and peas to dominate.

A Delicious Lunchtime Bread

And talking of breads, I have said elsewhere that one of my favourite weekend lunches is a selection of antipasti and freshly baked bread, so I couldn't let this book reach the printers without just one recipe for an olive oil bread that you can make at home. Ciabata is probably the best known of all Italian breads but it is not easy to make; the dough requires a complicated combination of kneading and twisting which is best done by a special commercial machine. Anyway, most supermarkets now stock very acceptable ciabatas that you finish in the oven at home, giving at least the illusion of being freshly baked. My recipe is for focaccia, a flat bread enriched with olive oil and crusted with coarsely ground sea salt. This is comparatively easy to make, although it requires a relatively long rising period because of the weight of the oil included in the dough. All sorts of toppings can be added – raw onions, anchovies, olives, sun-dried tomatoes; whatever you fancy, or whatever is in your store-cupboard. You might argue that bread is not really a lunch or supper dish – well, it doesn't fit neatly into any other section of this book and, when freshly baked, is so delicious that it is all too easy to make a complete meal out of a large portion of the loaf!

RED MULLET SALAD

Complemented by a marvellous fish sauce, red mullet fillets are served with diced tomatoes and a green salad

Serves 4

INGREDIENTS
12 small red mullet
30g/1oz butter
1 carrot, sliced
1 onion, sliced
60ml/2 fl oz white wine
Salt and freshly ground black
  pepper
4 tbsps olive oil
4 small servings mixed green
  salad
½ tbsp wine vinegar
1 tomato, seeded and diced
Small bunch chives

Gut and fillet the fish. Keep the heads and the bones. Set the fillets aside in a cool place until needed. Melt the butter in a frying pan and fry the carrot and onion for 1 minute, then stir in the heads and bones from the fish. Cook for 1 minute, stirring continuously. Deglaze the pan with the white wine, stir well until the wine has almost evaporated and then pour in 280ml/½ pint water. Cook for 15 minutes. Strain the sauce through a very fine sieve and reduce over a high heat to about 60ml/2 fl oz.

Season the mullet fillets with salt and pepper. Heat 2 tbsps olive oil in a frying pan and quickly fry the fillets on both sides for a few minutes. Drain the fillets on absorbent kitchen paper. Mix together the fish stock sauce, vinegar and the remaining olive oil. Taste and adjust the seasoning as necessary.

Place a little mixed green salad on 4 plates and sprinkle over the tomato. Finely chop almost all of the chives and mix them into the sauce. Place the warm fish fillets on the salad and pour over a little of the sauce. Decorate the plates with sprigs of chives.

GOAT'S CHEESE SALAD WITH TARRAGON

Goat's cheeses are traditional throughout the Mediterranean and many different cheeses are made. Most are soft but can be sliced for this dish. Very fresh cheeses can be too soft and rather watery.

Serves 4

INGREDIENTS
12 small slices white bread
4 small goat's cheeses (not too fresh)
4 small servings of mixed green salad
1 tbsp freshly chopped tarragon
1 tbsp tarragon vinegar
2 tbsps olive oil
Salt and freshly ground black pepper

Preheat the oven to 200˚C/400˚F/Gas Mark 6. Using a pastry cutter, cut the sliced bread into 12 rounds. Cut each cheese horizontally into 3 rounds and place on the prepared bread, then sprinkle with the chopped tarragon.

To prepare the dressing, mix together the tarragon vinegar, olive oil, salt and pepper. Stir or shake well and pour over the prepared mixed green salad. Place the cheese and bread rounds on a baking sheet in the preheated oven and cook until the cheese melts slightly and the top is golden – the cheese may be grilled, if you prefer. Remove from the oven and set the cheese and toast rounds on the tossed salad. Serve immediately.

CHICKEN LIVER SALAD

I prefer to serve this as a warm salad, with the livers freshly cooked on a bed of lettuce. If you prefer to serve the livers cold, allow them to cool in the vinaigrette before adding them to the salad leaves.

Serves 4

INGREDIENTS
4 slices white bread
90ml/3 fl oz olive oil
60g/2oz butter
12 chicken livers
1 shallot, finely chopped
2 cloves garlic, finely chopped
1 tbsp freshly chopped parsley
3 tbsps sherry or wine vinegar
4 small servings of shredded
   mixed green salad
Salt and freshly ground black
   pepper
1 tomato, cut into small dice

Cut the slices of bread into small, evenly-sized cubes. Heat 2 tbsps of the olive oil in a frying pan and quickly fry the bread cubes over a high heat. Fry until lightly golden and then drain on absorbent kitchen paper. Melt the butter in the same pan and gently fry the chicken livers.

Once the livers are cooked through (cut one to check that the centres are not too pink), add the shallot, garlic and parsley. Fry for a few minutes and then add 2 tbsps vinegar. Cook until it has almost evaporated, scraping up any sediment from the bottom of the pan.

Place the prepared green salad onto four plates and divide the livers evenly between the plates. Mix together the remaining vinegar, olive oil and a little salt and pepper. Shake or stir well to form a vinaigrette dressing. Scatter the diced tomato and the croûtons over the chicken livers and pour over a little dressing. The dish can be served immediately, or you may prefer to serve it when the livers are cold.

SEAFOOD TORTA

A torta is an Italian flan or tart. This one has a creamy
mixed fish filling and makes a splendid lunch or supper dish.

Serves 6-8

INGREDIENTS
Pastry
225g/8oz plain flour
Pinch of salt
120g/4oz unsalted butter
4 tbsps cold milk

Filling
120g/4oz white fish fillets (plaice,
 sole or cod)
150ml/¼ pint white wine
150ml/¼ pint water
Large pinch of dried hot pepper
 flakes
225g/8oz cooked prawns
120g/4oz crab meat
30g/1oz butter
30g/1oz flour
1 clove garlic, crushed
2 egg yolks
150ml/¼ pint double cream
Freshly chopped parsley
Salt and freshly ground black
 pepper

To prepare the pastry, sift the
flour and salt into a bowl, add
the butter in small pieces and rub
in until the mixture resembles
fine breadcrumbs – this may also
be done in a food processor. Mix
to a dough with the milk and
knead for about 1 minute. Leave
the dough in the refrigerator for
about 1 hour, wrapped in foil or
film.

To prepare the filling, cook the
white fish fillets in the water and
wine with the red pepper flakes
for about 6 minutes or until just
firm to the touch. When the fish
is cooked, remove it from the
liquid with a slotted spoon and
flake it into a bowl. Add the
prawns and the crab meat.
Reserve the cooking liquid. Melt
the butter in a small saucepan
and stir in the flour. Gradually
strain the cooking liquid from the
fish into the pan stirring
constantly until smooth. Add the
garlic, and bring to the boil
stirring constantly. Lower the
heat and allow the sauce to cook
for 1 minute. Add to the fish in
the bowl and set aside to cool.

Preheat the oven to
190°C/375°F/Gas Mark 5. Roll out
the pastry and use it to line a
20cm/8 inch flan tin. Prick the
base lightly with a fork and place
a sheet of greaseproof paper
inside. Fill with rice, dried beans
or baking beans and bake blind
for 15 minutes.

While the pastry is baking,
combine the egg yolks, cream
and parsley and stir into the fish
filling. Season with salt and
pepper. When the pastry is
cooked, remove the paper and
beans and pour in the filling.
Return the tart to the oven and
bake for a further 25 minutes.
Allow to cool slightly and then
remove from the tin. Transfer to
a serving dish and slice before
serving.

CHICK PEA SALAD

I often make a chick pea salad to serve as part of a mixed starter or antipasta. Use canned chick peas if you are short of time.

Serves 2-3

INGREDIENTS
300g/11oz chick peas
1 carrot, cut into 4
1 onion, stuck with 2 cloves
Sprig thyme
1 bay leaf
2 squid, cleaned and washed
1 tbsp freshly chopped parsley
1 clove garlic, chopped
1 shallot, chopped
1 tbsp wine vinegar
3 tbsps olive oil
Salt and freshly ground black
    pepper

Soak the chick peas overnight in plenty of cold water. Drain the chick peas and cook them in boiling salted water with the carrot, onion, thyme and the bay leaf. Cook for about 2 hours, until tender.

Cook the prepared squid in a steamer for approximately 4 minutes, then cut them into thin rounds. Make a sauce by mixing together all the remaining ingredients. When the peas are cooked through, remove the onion, carrot, bay leaf and thyme and discard them. Rinse the chick peas in cold water and set aside to drain. Once the chick peas are cold, combine them with the squid and the sauce. Serve at room temperature on small individual plates.

CHEESE FONDUE

Fondue originates just over the border in Switzerland, but this Italian version, using Fontina cheese and chives, is just that little bit different – try it!

Serves 4

INGREDIENTS

460g/1lb Fontina cheese
570ml/1 pint milk
4 slices white bread
2 tbsps oil
3 egg yolks
30g/1oz butter
Salt and freshly ground black pepper
3 tbsps freshly chopped chives

The day before serving the fondue, cut the cheese into small cubes, place in a bowl and cover with the milk (add more milk if required). Leave to soak overnight in a cool place.

The next day, cut the bread into small cubes and fry in the hot oil. About 10 minutes before serving the fondue, pour the cheese and milk mixture into a flameproof casserole, beat in the egg yolks and the butter and beat over a gentle heat until the cheese melts. Season with salt and pepper and serve immediately. Dip the cubes of bread into the mixture on long-handled fondue forks. Serve little plates of chopped chives around the table; dip the hot, cheese covered bread cubes in the chives.

POACHED EGGS IN BAROLO SAUCE

This is a most unusual recipe of eggs in a rich wine sauce.
Do try it – it's delicious

Serves 4

INGREDIENTS

420ml/¾ pint Barolo wine
2 shallots, finely chopped
3 large mushrooms, finely sliced
200ml/7 fl oz chicken stock
4 slices white bread
2 thick rashers bacon, cut into
   small cubes
60g/2oz butter
4 eggs
1 tbsp wine vinegar
Salt and freshly ground black
   pepper

Place the wine, shallots and mushrooms in a pan and reduce the liquid by three quarters over a high heat. Stir in the chicken stock and reduce again by half. Cut the slices of bread into either small rounds or squares and toast them under a hot grill. Set aside. Strain the reduced sauce through a very fine sieve into a clean saucepan. Add the bacon and cook over a moderate heat for 3 minutes. Whisk small pieces of the butter into the sauce until it is used up. Remove the pan from direct heat, but keep the sauce warm.

Poach the eggs in boiling water to which you have added the vinegar and a little salt. Drain the eggs once they are cooked to your liking on a clean tea towel and set on the toasts on a serving plate. Serve the eggs on the toasts with the sauce poured over.

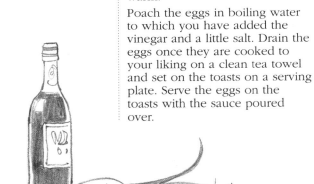

CHICKEN LIVERS WITH PEAS

Fresh garden peas are used as an ingredient in many Italian dishes rather than being served as a vegetable accompaniment. Here they are sautéed with chicken livers for an easy lunch or supper dish.

Serves 4

INGREDIENTS

340g/12oz chicken livers
460g/1lb shelled fresh green peas
60g/2oz butter
3 tbsps freshly chopped parsley
150ml/¼ pint chicken stock
4 slices of toast about 1.25cm/½
  inch thick
Salt

Clean the chicken livers and cut into halves or thirds. Cook the peas in lightly salted boiling water until tender but still firm (al dente). Melt 45g/1½oz of the butter in a saucepan, add the peas and parsley, then the chicken livers and stock. Stir well and cook for 5 minutes. Toast the bread, spread with the remaining butter, and place on individual plates. Remove the chicken livers and peas with a slotted spoon and spoon onto the toast. Keep warm. Boil the pan juices over a high heat, reducing to half their original volume. Season to taste with salt, then pour over chicken livers. Serve immediately.

STUFFED COURGETTES

Stuffed courgettes make attractive boat-shaped starters – I sometimes add a few peeled prawns to the filling mixture.

Serves 6

INGREDIENTS

1.6kg/3½lbs courgettes (12 small or 6 large)
90g/3oz ham, diced
2 tbsps freshly chopped parsley
Handful of freshly chopped basil leaves
2 tbsps dry breadcrumbs
120g/4oz grated Parmesan cheese
2 eggs, beaten
Nutmeg
Salt and freshly ground black pepper
90g/3oz butter, melted
1 tbsp flour
225ml/8 fl oz milk

Preheat the oven to 180°C/350°F/Gas Mark 4. Cut the ends off the courgettes and trim them to equal lengths. Wash and drain, then boil the courgettes in lightly salted water for 10 minutes or until half cooked. Drain. Slice in half lengthways and remove the pulp, reserving it in a bowl. Reserve the shells.

Mix the ham, parsley and basil with chopped courgette flesh, then add the breadcrumbs, all the grated Parmesan except for 2 tbsps, eggs, freshly grated nutmeg and salt and pepper to taste. Mix thoroughly and set aside. Melt half the butter and stir in the flour. Gradually add the milk, then stir over a low heat until the sauce boils and thickens. Stir the sauce into the courgette mixture, adding more breadcrumbs if the mixture is not thick enough to spoon. Using a spoon, fill the courgette shells with the filling. Arrange them side by side in a shallow baking dish buttered with the remaining butter. Sprinkle with the remaining grated Parmesan and bake in the preheated oven for 30 minutes. Serve hot.

ONION FOCACCIA

I find that focaccia is the easiest of the Italian breads to make at home – all you need is good olive oil and plenty of time. For a plain bread, omit the onions and top the loaf with plenty of coarsely ground sea salt.

Makes 1 loaf

INGREDIENTS
460g/1lb strong white flour
Pinch of salt
6 tbsps extra virgin olive oil
30g/1oz fresh yeast
225ml/8 fl oz warm water
2 large onions, finely sliced
Coarse sea salt and freshly
   ground black pepper

Mix the flour and salt in a bowl and make a well in the centre. Add 1 tbsp of the olive oil. Cream the yeast with a little of the warm water then add the remaining water and the yeast liquid to the flour. Mix to a manageable dough, adding a little more water if necessary. Turn onto a lightly floured surface and knead for 10-15 minutes, until the dough is smooth. Leave in a warm place in a covered oiled bowl for 1 hour, until well risen.

Scrape the dough from the bowl and knead it again until smooth.

Return the dough to the bowl and leave to rise for a further 1 hour. Place the sliced onions in cold water to soak – this makes them milder in flavour.

Preheat the oven to 220°C/425°F/Gas Mark 7. Scrape the dough from the bowl and knead again, then shape the dough to fit an oiled rectangular tin, approximately 25 x 30cm/10 x 12 inches. Press the dough into the corners of the tin and brush the remaining olive oil over the surface. Drain the onions and scatter them over the bread, then season the topping well with coarse sea salt and plenty of freshly ground black pepper.

Bake the focaccia in the preheated oven for 20-25 minutes – the base will sound hollow when the bread is cooked. Cool for 10 minutes or so, then slice the bread and serve.

PASTA

Although there is a companion volume to this book dealing purely with pasta, I felt that it would be impossible to produce a book on Classic Italian Cooking without some recipes for this popular Italian food. It is such an important part of the Italian cuisine, and one of the first foods that most of us bring to mind when thinking about Italian cooking.

The Pasta Revolution

This was not an ancient war, indeed it has only recently taken place. I'm talking about the tremendous move away from dried pasta to fresh, and especially to pasta made at home. This has definitely been made possible for most of us through the wide availability of a gadget, a pasta machine.

Pasta is traditionally made and rolled by hand. It is a time consuming and tricky process, requiring copious numbers of clean cloths to prevent the pasta sticking during rolling and drying, and a very large work surface – not to mention an extra long rolling pin! In the modern fitted kitchen, there simply isn't a surface large enough to roll out sufficient dough to feed a family, so the pasta rolling machine has been an absolute blessing for the would-be home pasta chef!

Just Flour and Eggs

The basic dough is just flour and eggs, although some people like to add a little olive oil for flavour. I would recommend that you add salt to the cooking water rather than to the dough as it can make the pasta tough if included. Salting the cooking water will help to bring out the eggy flavour of the pasta. Flavoured and coloured doughs may be made by using wholemeal flour, and by adding spinach, tomato or beetroot purée. The Italians even make a black pasta with squid ink.

Pasta Rollers

Most pasta machines are simply a pair of rollers which are adjusted throughout the rolling process, gradually making the dough thinner and thinner until the required thickness is achieved. Shapes from such machines are limited to flat strips of varying sizes; lasagne, tagliatelli and spaghetti. Tubes can be made with pasta extruders but these tend to be much noisier and rather less efficient, in my opinion, than a pasta roller.

Pasta may be cooked immediately after cutting but some people prefer to dry it for an hour or so before boiling. This is easiest over a broom handle kept specifically for the purpose and suspended between two work surfaces. However, mug trees provide a good alternative and dedicated pasta dryers, which look like multi-armed TV aerials, are now available and would make a good present for the keen cook who has every other piece of useful kitchen equipment!

Fresh may not be Best

I am definitely not a fan of commercially prepared fresh pasta, unless it comes from an Italian grocer where it is prepared daily on the premises. Other commercial fresh pastas tend to be far too thick, resulting in a tacky, stodgy dough when cooked. I would rather use a good quality dried pasta on the occasions when time does not allow me to make my own.

There are many, many pasta shapes – in fact there are far *too* many for them all to have specific sauce recipes. In this chapter I have included a selection of recipes that use the most common pasta shapes, those which you can buy easily in any grocer's shop or supermarket if you are not inclined to make your own dough.

Simple Rules for Success

There are a few basic rules which must be followed to obtain perfectly cooked pasta. They are:

- Always use as large a pan as possible to cook the pasta. This will prevent it from sticking together.
- Always salt the water, never add the salt to the dough.
- Have the water at a rolling boil before adding the pasta.
- Ensure that the water is boiling throughout the cooking period.
- Fresh pasta cooks very quickly, often in as short a time as two to three minutes. When it floats to the top of the pan it is a good indication that it is cooked.
- Pasta should be cooked *al dente*. This means just tender but still with a slight bite.
- Do not drain pasta too vigorously – this may cause it to stick together. Shake it gently in a colander to remove any surplus water.
- A little oil in the cooking water will help to prevent the pasta from sticking but I have found that the draining is the most critical thing to get right if the pasta is to stay separate.

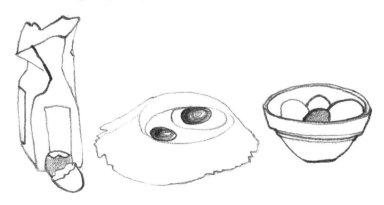

BASIC PASTA DOUGH

*Getting the correct consistency is the secret of pasta making –
too wet and the pasta will be sticky, too dry and it will
crumble apart. I always use size 2 eggs and find that they
give an excellent result.*

Serves 4-6

INGREDIENTS
460g/1lb strong plain white flour
4 eggs, lightly beaten
Olive oil or water, if necessary

Place the flour in a large mixing
bowl, make a well in the centre
and add the eggs. Mix together
well, using a fork or your fingers,
until the dough can be gathered
up into a ball. If the dough is too
dry, add a few drops of water or
olive oil.

Turn the dough out onto a board
and knead well for 5-10 minutes,
until it is smooth, shiny and no
longer sticky. Cover with cling
film and leave to rest in a cool
place for 30 minutes before
rolling out and shaping as
required.

WHOLEWHEAT PASTA

Use a fine wholewheat flour to make a brown pasta with flavour, it bears none of the resemblance to cardboard that commercial wholewheat pasta sometimes exhibits.

Serves 4

INGREDIENTS
280g/10oz plain wholewheat flour
3 eggs, beaten
1 tbsp olive oil

Place the flour in a large mixing bowl, make a well in the centre and add the eggs and olive oil. Mix together with a fork until the dough can be gathered into a ball. If the dough is too dry and will not come together, add a few drops of water.

Knead the dough for 5-10 minutes, incorporating all the flour on the board, until is is smooth, shiny and no longer sticky. Cover with cling film and leave to rest in a cool place for 30 minutes. Roll out and shape the pasta as required.

SPINACH PASTA

Pasta verde is not musical, it is green, being flavoured with a spinach purée. Use this pasta with peppery sauces and for dishes that require extra colour.

Serves 4

INGREDIENTS
280g/10oz fine plain wholewheat
  flour
2 eggs, lightly beaten
120g/4oz cooked spinach, finely
  chopped
1 tbsp olive oil

Place the flour in a large mixing bowl and make a well in the centre. Mix the eggs with the spinach and pour into the centre of the flour with the olive oil. Mix together with a fork until the dough can be gathered into a ball. Add a little water or extra oil if the dough is too dry. Knead lightly until the dough is smooth, shiny and no longer sticky. Wrap in cling film and rest in a cool place for 30 minutes before rolling out and shaping as required.

LASAGNE

Lasagne, a glorious dish of layered pasta, meat sauce and fragrant white sauce, is best made with fresh pasta. If using dried, chose a lasagne which requires pre-cooking – it only takes a few minutes and the flavour is so much better than the no-cook variety.

Serves 4

INGREDIENTS
8 sheets lasagne

Meat Sauce
60g/2oz butter or margarine
1 onion, chopped
1 stick celery, sliced
1 carrot, diced
120g/4oz minced beef
1 tbsp flour
1 tbsp tomato purée
150ml/¼ pint beef stock
1 tsp freshly chopped marjoram
Salt and freshly ground black
  pepper.

Béchamel Sauce
280ml/½ pint milk
6 black peppercorns
Slice of onion
1 bay leaf
Parsley stalks
60g/2oz butter or margarine
45g/1½oz flour

Prepare the meat sauce. Heat the butter in a pan and add the onion, celery and carrot, cook until the onion is golden. Add the minced beef and brown well, then stir in the flour; add the tomato purée, beef stock, marjoram, salt and pepper. Simmer for 15 minutes.

Meanwhile, cook the lasagne in plenty of boiling salted water for 10 minutes, or until tender. Rinse in cold water and drain carefully. Lay the lasagne out on a clean cloth to dry.

Prepare the béchamel sauce. Bring the milk almost to the boil in a saucepan with the peppercorns, onion, bay leaf and parsley stalks and remove from the heat. Allow to cool for 5 minutes, then strain through a sieve to remove the flavourings. Melt the butter in a saucepan, then stir in the flour and cook for 30 seconds. Remove the pan from the heat and gradually add the milk, stirring continuously. Bring to the boil, then simmer for 3 minutes.

Grease an ovenproof baking dish. Line the base with a layer of lasagne. Cover with a layer of meat sauce, then a layer of béchamel sauce. Add another layer of lasagne, repeating the layers until all the ingredients are used, finishing with a layer of béchamel sauce. Bake in the preheated oven for about 20 minutes, or until the top is golden. Serve immediately.

BEANY LASAGNE

Lasagne makes an ideal dish for vegetarians. Vegetarian lasagne usually contains lentils but this recipe is made with aduki beans, giving a nutty flavour and texture.

Serves 4-6

INGREDIENTS
8 sheets wholewheat lasagne
1 large onion, finely chopped
1 tbsp olive oil
1-2 cloves garlic, crushed
225g/8oz aduki beans, cooked
1 green pepper, seeded and
    chopped
400g/14oz can chopped tomatoes
1 tbsp tomato purée
1 tsp dried basil
1 tsp dried oregano
Salt and freshly ground black
    pepper

Sauce
30g/1oz margarine or butter
30g/1oz plain wholewheat flour
420ml/¾ pint milk
60g/2oz Cheddar cheese, grated
    (optional)
Salt and freshly ground black
    pepper

Cook the lasagne in a large pan of boiling, salted water for 8-10 minutes. Drain well and spread out on clean cloths until required. Cook the onion in the oil until soft but not browned. Add the crushed garlic, then the beans, green pepper, chopped tomatoes, tomato purée and herbs. Season and simmer for about 10 minutes, or until the vegetables are tender.

Preheat the oven to 180°C/350°F/Gas Mark 4. To make the sauce, combine the margarine, flour and cold milk. Gradually bring to the boil, stirring continuously. When thickened, allow to simmer slowly for approximately 6 minutes, then stir in the cheese and season to taste. Spoon half the bean and vegetable mixture into a greased ovenproof dish and top with half the lasagne. Repeat the layers and top with the cheese sauce. Bake in the preheated oven for 35 minutes, or until golden brown and bubbling. Serve immediately.

COURGETTE AND PINE NUT LASAGNE WITH AUBERGINE SAUCE

Not all lasagnes are made with a meat sauce – this delicious variation is light and fragrant. It is a perfect vegetarian party dish.

Serves 4

INGREDIENTS
12 sheets wholewheat lasagne
90g/3oz pine nuts
30g/1oz butter
680g/1½lbs courgettes, trimmed
   and sliced
280g/10oz Ricotta cheese
½ tsp nutmeg
1 tbsp olive oil
1 large aubergine, sliced
150ml/¼ pint water
Salt and freshly ground black
   pepper
90g/3oz Cheddar cheese, grated

Preheat the oven to 190°C/375°F/Gas Mark 5. Cook the lasagne in plenty of boiling salted water for 8-10 minutes, then drain and leave on clean cloths until required. Place the pine nuts in a dry pan and roast gently over a low heat for 2 minutes. Set to one side. Melt the butter and cook the courgettes, with a little water if necessary, until just tender. Combine the courgettes, pine nuts and ricotta cheese, then add the nutmeg and mix thoroughly.

Heat the olive oil in a separate pan and cook the aubergine for 4 minutes. Add the water and simmer, covered, until soft. Season with salt and pepper. Blend in a liquidiser or food processor until smooth, adding a little extra water if necessary.

Place 4 strips of lasagne in the bottom of a greased ovenproof dish and top with half the courgette mixture. Place 4 more strips of lasagne over the courgettes and add the aubergine sauce followed by the remaining courgettes. Cover with the remaining lasagne and the rest of the sauce. Top with the grated cheese and bake for 40 minutes, until the cheese is golden brown.

85

SPAGHETTI BOLOGNESE

This must surely be one of the most famous dishes in the world – it is certainly one of the most copied and abused! I hope you like this version.

Serves 4

INGREDIENTS
30g/1oz butter or margarine
1 tbsp olive oil
2 onions, finely chopped
1 carrot, diced
225g/8oz minced beef
120g/4oz can tomato purée
Salt and freshly ground black
  pepper
280ml/½ pint brown beef stock
2 tbsps sherry
280g/10oz spaghetti
Parmesan cheese

Heat the butter and oil in a pan and cook the onions and carrot slowly until soft. Increase the heat and add the minced beef. Fry for a few minutes, then stir, and continue cooking until the meat is browned all over. Add the tomato purée, salt and pepper and the stock. Simmer gently for about 45 minutes, stirring occasionally, until the mixture thickens. Add the sherry to the sauce and cook for a further 5 minutes. Meanwhile, bring a large pan of salted water to the boil, add the spaghetti and cook for 10 minutes, or until *al dente*. Drain. Serve the spaghetti with the Bolognese sauce and grated Parmesan cheese.

SPAGHETTI MARINARA

I always enjoy a fish sauce with pasta – it makes a change from the more traditional meat sauces and is slightly lighter. This is one of my favourite summer recipes.

Serves 4

INGREDIENTS
60g/2oz can anchovy fillets
5 tbsps water
5 tbsps dry white wine
1 bay leaf
4 peppercorns
225g/8oz scallops, cleaned and
  sliced
2 tbsps olive oil
2 cloves garlic, crushed
1 tbsp freshly chopped basil
400g/14oz can chopped tomatoes
1 tbsp tomato purée
280g/10oz spaghetti
460g/1lb cooked prawns, shelled
  and de-veined
2 tbsps freshly chopped parsley
Salt and freshly ground black
  pepper

Drain anchovies and cut them into small pieces. Place the water, wine, bay leaf and peppercorns in a pan, and bring to a slow boil. Add the scallops and poach for 2 minutes. Remove the scallops with a slotted spoon and drain.

Heat the oil in a separate pan, add the garlic and basil, and cook for 30 seconds. Add the tomatoes, chopped anchovies and tomato purée. Stir until combined, then cook for 10 minutes.

Meanwhile, bring a large pan of salted water to the boil, add the spaghetti and cook for 10 minutes, or until *al dente*. Drain. Add the prawns and scallops to the sauce, and cook a further 1 minute. Add 1 tbsp of parsley and stir. Season with salt and pepper to taste. Pour the sauce over the spaghetti and serve immediately, sprinkled with the remaining parsley.

SPAGHETTI WITH BASIL AND TOMATO SAUCE

This dish is delicious in its simplicity. The flavours of the tomatoes and basil really shine through.

Serves 4

460g/1lb spaghetti
3 tbsps olive oil
1 clove garlic, chopped
3 tomatoes, peeled, seeded and chopped
Salt and freshly ground black pepper
10 fresh basil leaves, finely chopped

Cook the spaghetti to your liking in boiling salted water. Rinse and drain.

Heat the olive oil in a frying pan and cook the garlic, tomato, salt and pepper over a gentle heat for 10-12 minutes, stirring frequently. Stir the well drained pasta into the sauce, mix well and re-heat the spaghetti. Just before serving, stir in the finely chopped basil, season with extra salt and pepper if necessary and serve.

SPAGHETTI WITH KIDNEY BEANS AND PESTO

Pesto is a glorious Italian sauce of basil, garlic and pine nuts blended with olive oil – if often has Parmesan and Pecorino cheese added to it as well. Store the sauce in a screw-top jar in the refrigerator for up to a week, and add the sauce to pasta, rice and meat dishes.

Serves 4

INGREDIENTS
Pesto Sauce
1 large bunch fresh basil
4 cloves garlic, crushed
3 tbsps pine nuts
150ml/¼ pint extra virgin olive oil
1 tbsp lemon juice
Salt and freshly ground black pepper

225g/8oz spaghetti
1 small onion, finely chopped
2 tbsps olive oil
1 clove garlic, crushed
225g/8oz red kidney beans, cooked, or 420g/15oz can, drained
Sprigs of fresh basil, to garnish

Prepare the sauce. Place all the ingredients in a liquidiser or processor and blend until fairly smooth; the sauce should retain a little texture.

Bring a large pan of salted water to the boil, add the spaghetti and cook for 10 minutes or until *al dente*. Meanwhile, fry the onion gently in the olive oil for 3 minutes, mix in the garlic and 2 tsps of the pesto sauce. Drain the spaghetti thoroughly and add it to the onion and pesto mixture, together with the red kidney beans. Stir over a gentle heat for 1-2 minutes, then serve piping hot, garnished with basil.

SPAGHETTI WITH SORREL AND CHEESE SAUCE

Sorrel is very similar to spinach, a vegetable that is used extensively in Italian cookery. In this recipe it produces a delicious and unusual dish.

Serves 4

INGREDIENTS

460g/1lb freshly cooked
   spaghetti
120g/4oz sorrel
280ml/½ pint chicken or
   vegetable stock
15g/½oz butter or margarine
1 tbsp flour
120ml/4 fl oz double cream
60g/2oz grated Pecorino cheese
Salt and freshly ground black
   pepper
Pinch of cayenne pepper
2 hard-boiled eggs, roughly
   chopped
Parmesan cheese

Cook the spaghetti to your liking. Discard any thick stems from the sorrel, then cook the leaves in the stock for 4 minutes. Melt the butter in a separate saucepan and stir in the flour. Purée the sorrel in its stock in a liquidiser or food processor and add the purée to the saucepan. Bring to the boil, stirring constantly. Once the sauce has thickened, stir in the cream, salt, cheese, pepper and cayenne pepper and carefully stir in the eggs. Heat the sauce gently, pour it over the pasta and add grated Parmesan cheese before serving.

MEAT RAVIOLI

*Ravioli are little parcels of pasta traditionally filled with
meat. Homemade ravioli bears little resemblance to the
rather nondescript ravioli sold in cans – do try this recipe.*

Serves 4

INGREDIENTS
Filling
60g/2oz butter or margarine
1 clove garlic, crushed
1 onion, grated
225g/8oz minced beef
5 tbsps red wine
Salt and freshly ground black
  pepper
2 tbsps breadcrumbs
120g/4oz cooked spinach,
  chopped
2 eggs, beaten

Dough
250g/9oz strong plain flour
3 eggs, lightly beaten

Sauce
400g/14oz can chopped tomatoes
1 small onion, grated
1 small carrot, finely diced
1 bay leaf
3 parsley stalks
Salt and freshly ground black
  pepper
60g/2oz Parmesan cheese

Prepare the filling. Heat the butter
in a pan, add the garlic and onion,
and fry gently for 1 minute. Add
the minced beef, and fry until
browned, then add the red wine,
salt and pepper and cook,
uncovered, for 15 minutes. Strain
the juices and reserve them for the
sauce. Allow the filling to cool,
then add the breadcrumbs, chopped spinach, and beaten eggs to
bind. Add salt and pepper to taste.

To make the dough, sieve the
flour into a bowl. Make a well in
the centre and add the eggs.
Work the flour and eggs together
with a fork, then knead by hand,
until a smooth dough is formed.
Wrap the dough in plastic film
and leave to rest for 15 minutes
in a cool place. Lightly flour a
board, and roll the dough out
thinly into a rectangle. Cut the
dough in half.

Place small piles of the filling
about 4cm/1½ inches apart on
one half of the dough. Place the
remaining dough on top and cut
with a ravioli cutter or small
pastry cutter. Seal the edges by
pinching together.

Cook the ravioli in batches in a
large, wide pan with plenty of
boiling, salted water until tender
– about 8 minutes. Remove the
ravioli carefully with a slotted
spoon.

To make the sauce, place all the
ingredients in a saucepan. Add
the reserved juice from the
cooked meat, and bring to the
boil. Simmer for 10 minutes.
Press the sauce through a sieve,
and return the smooth sauce to
the pan. Adjust the seasoning.
Place the ravioli in a warmed
serving dish and cover with the
tomato sauce. Serve immediately
with grated Parmesan cheese.

RAVIOLI WITH RICOTTA CHEESE

*Ravioli are traditionally filled with meat but cheese fillings
are also popular. Ricotta is the best cheese to use and is
available in most supermarkets.*

Serves 4

INGREDIENTS
Filling
30g/1oz butter or margarine
1 egg yolk
225g/8oz Ricotta cheese
60g/2oz Parmesan cheese, grated
2 tbsps freshly chopped parsley
Salt and freshly ground black
  pepper

Dough
250g/9oz strong plain flour
3 eggs, lightly beaten

Tomato Sauce
1 tbsp olive oil
30g/1oz bacon
1 small onion, chopped
1 bay leaf
1 tbsp freshly chopped basil
1 tbsp flour
400g/14oz can chopped tomatoes
Salt and freshly ground black
  pepper
1 tbsp double cream

To make the filling, cream the butter, add the egg yolk, and beat well. Beat the Ricotta cheese to a cream, and add the butter and egg mixture gradually, beating until smooth. Add the Parmesan cheese and parsley, and salt and pepper to taste. Set to one side.

Prepare the dough by sifting the flour into a bowl. Make a well in the centre, and add the eggs. Work the flour and eggs together with a fork, and then knead the dough by hand until smooth.

Wrap in plastic film and leave to rest for 15 minutes in a cool place. Lightly flour a board, and roll the dough out thinly into a rectangle. Cut the dough in half.

Shape the filling into small balls and set them about 4cm/1½ inches apart on one half of the dough. Place the remaining dough on top and cut with a ravioli cutter or small pastry cutter. Seal the edges with a fork or the fingertips. Cook the ravioli in batches in a large, wide pan with plenty of boiling, salted water until tender – about 8 minutes. Remove the ravioli carefully with a slotted spoon.

While the pasta is cooking, prepare the sauce. Heat the oil, and fry the bacon and onion until golden. Add the bay leaf and basil, and stir in the flour. Cook for 1 minute, then add the tomatoes off the heat, stirring continuously, with salt and pepper to taste. Return the pan to the heat and bring to the boil. Cook for 5 minutes, then press the sauce through a sieve. Stir in the cream, and adjust the seasoning to taste.

Pour the tomato sauce over the ravioli parcels, toss gently and serve immediately.

TAGLIATELLE WITH BACON AND TOMATO SAUCE

A simple but delicious dish that can be made in minutes.

Serves 4

INGREDIENTS
1 tbsp olive oil
1 onion, finely chopped
6 rashers of bacon, cut into strips
2 tbsps freshly chopped parsley
2 tbsps freshly chopped basil
400g/14oz can chopped tomatoes
Salt and freshly ground black
  pepper
280g/10oz tagliatelle
60g/2oz Pecorino cheese

Heat the oil in a large pan, add the onion and bacon and cook gently until the onion is soft but not browned. Add the parsley, basil and tomatoes and simmer gently for 5 minutes, stirring occasionally, then season to taste with salt and pepper.

Meanwhile, cook the tagliatelle in a large pan of boiling salted water. Cook for about 10 minutes, until *al dente*. Drain the pasta and return it to the pan. Add the sauce and toss thoroughly. Serve with grated Pecorino cheese.

TAGLIATELLE WITH PINE NUTS

This is a piquant recipe, suitable for vegetarians, but popular with meat eaters too! The pine nuts give a slightly crunchy texture to the dish.

Serves 4

INGREDIENTS
340g/12oz tagliatelle
Salt
90ml/3 fl oz olive oil
1 large onion, sliced
1 clove garlic, crushed
120g/4oz pine nuts
400g/14oz can artichoke hearts,
  drained
2 tbsps freshly chopped parsley
Parmesan cheese

Cook the tagliatelle in plenty of lightly salted boiling water for 10 minutes or until *al dente*. Just before the tagliatelle is cooked, heat the oil in a frying pan and fry the onion and garlic until starting to brown. Add the pine nuts and cook for 1 minute, then add the artichoke hearts and parsley. Heat gently for a few minutes.

Drain the tagliatelle well and add it to the pan; toss until the tagliatelle is well coated in the oil. Stir in a generous handful of grated Parmesan cheese.

Transfer to a warmed serving dish and scatter with a little more grated Parmesan. Serve immediately.

HOME-MADE TAGLIATELLE WITH SUMMER SAUCE

This is a very unusual recipe. The sauce is cold and is best prepared the day before it is required, to allow the flavours to blend. The pasta is made with some semolina, which gives it an interesting, grainy texture.

Serves 4

INGREDIENTS

Sauce

460g/1lb tomatoes, seeded and cut into small dice
1 large green pepper, seeded and cut into small dice
1 onion, finely chopped
1 tbsp freshly chopped basil
1 tbsp freshly chopped parsley
2 cloves garlic, crushed
150ml/¼ pint olive oil

Pasta Dough

120g/4oz plain flour
120g/4oz fine semolina
2 large eggs, lightly beaten
2 tsps olive oil

Combine all the sauce ingredients, mixing well. Cover and refrigerate for as long as possible, preferably overnight.

Mix the flour and semolina in a bowl and make a well in the centre. Add the eggs and oil and mix to a dough with a fork. Bring the dough together with your hands and knead firmly on a lightly floured surface until smooth and shiny. Cover the dough with plastic film and leave it to rest for 15 minutes in a cool place.

Divide the dough in four and roll out thinly with a rolling pin on a floured surface or use a pasta machine, dusting the dough lightly with flour before rolling. If using a machine, follow the manufacturer's directions. Allow the sheets of pasta to dry for about 10 minutes on clean cloths. Cut the sheets into strips about 6mm/¼ inch wide, dusting lightly with flour while cutting. Leave the cut pasta to dry for 10 minutes or so.

Cook the pasta for 5-6 minutes in boiling salted water with a spoonful of oil. Drain the pasta and rinse under very hot water. Toss in a colander to drain excess water. Place the hot pasta in a serving dish, add the cold sauce and toss before serving.

CARRETTIERA WITH TAGLIATELLE

Tuna and tagliatelle – two popular Italian ingredients that are just meant for each other.

Serves 4

INGREDIENTS
250g/9oz tagliatelle
60g/2oz butter or margarine
120g/4oz mushrooms, cleaned
  and sliced
200g/7oz can tuna fish, flaked
Salt and freshly ground black
  pepper

Bring a large pan of salted water to the boil, add the tagliatelle and cook for 10 minutes, or until *al dente*.

Melt the butter in a pan, add the mushrooms and cook for 4-5 minutes, then add the tuna and cook for a further 5 minutes. Drain the tagliatelle and add it to the mushrooms and tuna. Season with salt and pepper and serve immediately.

TAGLIATELLE PESCATORE

Preparing the seafood can be time-consuming, but the results justify the effort!

Serves 3-4

INGREDIENTS
150ml/¼ pint mussels
150ml/¼ pint clams
225g/8oz cod fillets
120g/4oz squid, cleaned
4 king prawns, cooked
4 fresh oysters, cooked
225g/8oz tagliatelle
4 tbsps olive oil
225ml/8 fl oz dry white wine
700ml/1¼ pints tomato sauce or
  passata
2 tbsps tomato purée
½ green pepper, diced
Salt and freshly ground black
  pepper

Prepare the seafood. If using fresh mussels, clean them, removing any beards, and cook in boiling water for 3 minutes until they open. (Discard any that remain closed.) Cool and remove the mussels from their shells, keeping a few in shells for garnish if desired. Skin the cod fillets, and cut into 1.25cm/½ inch pieces. Clean the squid and cut into rings.

Heat 2 tbsps of the oil in a pan, and add the squid. Fry gently until golden brown, then add the wine, tomato, green pepper, and salt and pepper to taste. Simmer for 20 minutes then add the cod. Simmer for a further 10 minutes, stirring occasionally. Add the clams and mussels and, when the sauce returns to the boil, adjust the seasoning.

Meanwhile, cook the tagliatelle in plenty of boiling salted water for 10 minutes, or until *al dente*. Drain well. Add the seafood, and toss until well mixed. Garnish with the king prawns and oysters, and serve hot.

FARFALLE WITH CREAMY CHEESE SAUCE

Pasta in cheese sauce has long been a favourite supper dish in our house – the farfalle gives this simple dish a most attractive appearance.

Serves 4

INGREDIENTS
15g/½oz butter or margarine
15g/½oz flour
280ml/½ pint milk
60g/2oz Gruyère or Cheddar
  cheese, grated
½ tsp French mustard
280g/10oz farfalle (pasta bows)
1 tbsp grated Parmesan

Heat the butter in a pan. Stir in the flour and cook for 1 minute. Remove the pan from the heat and gradually stir in the milk. Return the pan to the heat and stir continuously until the sauce boils. Boil for 3 minutes, then stir in the Gruyère or Cheddar cheese and mustard.

Meanwhile, cook the pasta in plenty of boiling salted water for 10 minutes, or until *al dente*. Rinse in hot water and drain well. Pour the cheese sauce over the pasta and toss. Top with a sprinkling of Parmesan cheese. Serve immediately.

MACARONI WITH BASIL AND WALNUT SAUCE

Walnuts give a wonderful flavour to pasta – this dish has long been a favourite in our house but I have to confess to adding rather more garlic than is suggested here!

Serves 4

INGREDIENTS
120g/4oz shelled walnuts
15 basil leaves
¼ clove garlic
460g/1lb macaroni
Salt and freshly ground black pepper
1 drop olive oil
60g/2oz butter

Pound together the walnuts, basil leaves and garlic in a pestle and mortar until a smooth paste is formed.

Cook the pasta in boiling salted water for 10 minutes or until *al dente*. Rinse in hot water and set aside to drain.

Heat the olive oil and butter together in a saucepan, add the basil, walnut and garlic mixture and stir well to combine all the ingredients. Add the drained macaroni to the pan, stir well and heat through. Check the seasoning, add salt and pepper as necessary, and serve immediately.

FUSILLI CARBONARA

*Carbonara is one of my favourite pasta sauces – rich,
creamy and tangy. I sometimes add garlic – this recipe adds
a few capers.*

Serves 4

INGREDIENTS
460g/1lb fusilli
60ml/2 fl oz milk
150ml/¼ pint single cream
Salt and freshly ground black
    pepper
2 rashers bacon, cut into small
    pieces
1 tbsp capers
4 egg yolks

Cook the fusilli in boiling salted water. Drain, rinse in hot water and set aside to drain thoroughly.

Heat the milk and cream in a saucepan. Season with salt and pepper, then add the bacon and the capers and cook for 1 minute. Add the drained fusilli and cook until heated through completely. Beat the egg yolks in a small bowl and then add them to the hot fusilli. Remove the saucepan from the heat, stirring continuously with a wooden spoon, and serve. The egg yolks will cook in the heat from the fusilli.

CANNELLONI

Cannelloni should be cooked in a very hot oven to crisp the top of the pasta, whilst leaving most of the dish tender and moist.

Serves 4

INGREDIENTS
Filling
1 tbsp olive oil
2 cloves garlic, crushed
1 onion, chopped
460g/1lb minced beef
1 tsp tomato purée
1 tbsp freshly chopped basil
1 tbsp freshly chopped oregano
225g/8oz frozen spinach, thawed
1 egg, lightly beaten
4 tbsps double cream
Salt and freshly ground black
    pepper

12 cannelloni tubes
2 tbsps Parmesan cheese, grated
1 tbsp oil

Tomato Sauce
1 tbsp olive oil
1 onion, chopped
1 clove garlic, crushed
400g/14oz can chopped tomatoes
2 tbsps tomato purée
Salt and freshly ground black
    pepper

Béchamel Sauce
280ml/½ pint milk
1 slice of onion
3 peppercorns
1 small bay leaf
30g/1oz butter or margarine
30g/1oz flour
Salt and freshly ground black
    pepper

Prepare the filling. Heat the oil in a pan, and fry the garlic and onion until soft and transparent. Add the beef and cook, stirring continuously, until well browned.

Drain off any fat, add the tomato purée, basil and oregano, and cook gently for 15 minutes. Add the spinach, egg and cream, and salt and pepper to taste.

Cook the cannelloni in a large pan of boiling, salted water for 15-20 minutes, until tender. Rinse in hot water and drain.

Carefully fill the tubes with the meat mixture, using a piping bag or a teaspoon.

Preheat the oven to 230°C/450°F/ Gas Mark 8. Make the tomato sauce. Heat the oil in pan, add the onion and garlic, and cook gently until transparent. Press the tomatoes through a sieve, and add to the pan with the tomato purée, salt and pepper. Bring to the boil, and then simmer for 5 minutes. Set to one side.

To make the béchamel sauce, place the milk in a pan with the onion, peppercorns and bay leaf. Heat gently for 1 minute, taking care not to boil, and set aside to cool for 5 minutes. Strain. Melt the butter in a pan. Remove it from the heat and stir in the flour, then gradually add the milk. Bring to the boil, stirring continuously, until the sauce thickens. Season to taste.

Spread the tomato sauce in the base of an ovenproof dish. Lay the cannelloni on top, and cover with the béchamel sauce. Sprinkle with the cheese, and bake for 10-15 minutes.

PASTA SHELLS WITH
MUSHROOM SAUCE

*This tasty mushroom sauce makes a perfect supper dish
poured over pasta. I sometimes add a pinch of ground
mace to the sauce – add it to the mushrooms while they
are cooking.*

Serves 4

INGREDIENTS
225g/8oz button mushrooms
30g/1oz butter or margarine
30g/1oz flour
570ml/1 pint milk
Salt and freshly ground black
  pepper
280g/10oz pasta shells

Rinse the mushrooms and chop them roughly. Melt the butter in a saucepan and add the mushrooms. Fry for 5 minutes, stirring occasionally. Stir in the flour and cook for 1 minute. Draw the pan off the heat, and add the milk gradually, stirring continuously. Return to the heat and bring to the boil and cook for 3 minutes, stirring continuously. Season with salt and pepper.

Meanwhile, cook the pasta shells in plenty of boiling, salted water for 10 minutes, or until *al dente*. Rinse in hot water and drain well.

Place in a warmed serving dish, and add the mushroom sauce. Serve immediately.

PENNE WITH ANCHOVY SAUCE

This is an unusual sauce but one which makes good use of the favourite Italian ingredient, the anchovy.

Serves 4

INGREDIENTS
6-8 anchovy fillets, drained
2 tbsps olive oil
400g/14oz can chopped tomatoes
3 tbsps freshly chopped parsley
Freshly ground black pepper
280g/10oz penne
30g/1oz butter or margarine,
    melted
30g/1oz Parmesan cheese

Chop the anchovies and cook them briefly in the oil, stirring until they break up into a paste. Add the chopped tomatoes with the parsley and freshly ground black pepper to taste. Bring to the boil and simmer, uncovered for 10 minutes.

Meanwhile, cook the penne in plenty of boiling salted water for 10 minutes or until *al dente*. Rinse in hot water and drain well, then toss the penne in the melted butter. Combine the sauce with the pasta, sprinkle with some extra chopped parsley, and serve immediately with a little grated Parmesan cheese.

RICE, PIZZAS & PANCAKES

The inclusion of this chapter leaves no doubt that this is a book on classic Italian cookery! These are foods which, with pasta, have come to symbolise, rightly or wrongly, the food of Italy.

Risotto – a Creamy Taste Sensation

When I was at college risotto was *the* trendy food – it seemed almost to have been invented by a newly adventurous generation of package-deal travellers. Unfortunately, they came back with the wrong recipe! The risottos that I was introduced to were made with wonderfully separate grains of long-grain rice and the most important aim seemed to be to make the dish as colourful as possible. Vegetables and fruit were therefore included and most risottos were packed full of chopped ham, carrots, lightly-cooked peppers, green beans and lots of canned pineapple chunks. The finished dish was often so dry that a sauce, if not a gravy, was called for! And that's how I thought risotto was meant to be!

Of course, on my very first eating trip to Italy I discovered that true risotto bears no resemblance at all to the popular misconception of the early 1970s. My first Italian risotto, enjoyed in a popular restaurant in Parma, the gastronomic capital of northern Italy, was rich, creamy and moist – indeed, almost wet. It was also a dull green in colour with little texture other than the *al dente* rice, being flavoured almost exclusively with pesto. Above all, it was one of those most heavenly of taste sensations where the first mouthful induces an almost total state of relaxation and temporary loss of control of the spine through sheer and utter pleasure – it was truly memorable.

One of the most important ingredients for recreating the authentic Italian risotto is to use the correct rice. Risotto rice is a short, long-grain – that is, shorter and rounder than long-grain, but longer and thinner than short-grain! Confused? Well, not to worry, because the rice is very clearly labelled and is available now in most supermarkets as part of their range of speciality rices. If you visit a good delicatessen or Italian grocers you should be able to purchase arborio rice, which is the finest grade of risotto rice. I have referred to the rice used in the following recipes as arborio, but the risotto rice from supermarkets will also give satisfactory results. Some of the best rice in Italy is grown in the Po valley.

Pizzas – a Medley of Tempting Meals

Pizzas are the sort of food that you 'pop out for', 'stop off for' or 'grab'. In short, to most of us they are almost a convenience or fast food; quick, tasty and satisfying. One of my favourite chains of pizza restaurants has a branch right on my route home from London with parking outside the door – it is a favourite and much-used refreshment point!

If you have the time to make your own dough, then of course the pizza will be much better than anything produced on a production line. I prefer to use fresh yeast for the base but the easy-blend, one-rising variety also produces good results, especially if you are in a hurry. The dough can be mixed, shaped in the tin and left for its only rising while you prepare the topping. I am a fan of thin crust pizzas and find that the thick or deep crust varieties are simply too filling. In consequence, I find that even a large home-made pizza to cut for eight people will be cooked in little more than twenty minutes if it has a thin crust.

Crespelle and Gnocchi – Parcels of Pleasure

One filled, one coated with sauce – both crespelle and gnocchi are typically Italian and delicious! Crespelle are thin pancakes, cooked, stuffed and then lightly baked or grilled just to crisp the tops before serving. Gnocchi are small balls of dough, made from a potato base or from semolina, and either fried or boiled and served with a sauce. Perhaps an inexperienced gnocchi cook might try to serve them as a pasta or potato substitute, as a side dish to meat or fish, but I find this too much. Gnocchi should be light in texture but they are often very rich and stand alone as a course in their own right. Prepared gnocchi are available but they are definitely not on my shopping list – you simply cannot beat home-made ones! To achieve evenly-sized gnocchi, place the dough in a forcing bag fitted with a large plain pipe and squeeze out small amounts, matching the shape and size of the pieces.

MUSSEL RISOTTO

Mussels and risotto are two of my favourite foods! This recipe is my idea of heaven.

Serves 4

INGREDIENTS
1.14 litres/2 pints small mussels
1 shallot, chopped
120ml/4 fl oz white wine
60g/2oz butter
1 onion, chopped
460g/1lb arborio rice
Powdered saffron
Salt and freshly ground black
  pepper

Clean the mussels under plenty of running water, scraping and brushing off any sand and grit, and removing any beards. Place the clean mussels in a large saucepan with the shallot and the wine. Cover and cook over a high heat until the mussels open. Cover, and set the saucepan aside to allow the mussels to cool. Once they are cool, remove the mussels from their shells. Strain the cooking juices through a fine sieve which has been covered with a muslin. Discard all but the juice and the mussels.

Preheat the oven to 200°C/400°F/ Gas Mark 6. Melt the butter in a frying pan and gently fry the onion and the rice. Fry until the rice is transparent (approximately 1 minute), then pour in the cooking juices made up to 700ml/1¼ pints with water. Stir in 2 to 3 pinches of saffron, just enough to slightly colour the liquid. Transfer to an ovenproof dish, season with salt and pepper and stir in the mussels. Cover and cook in the preheated oven for approximately 20 minutes until the rice is tender but not soft. Serve hot.

TRUFFLE RISOTTO

*Truffles have a rich and pungent flavour – two truffles will
adequately season this delicious risotto. Serve with a few
parings of Parmesan cheese if you wish.*

Serves 4

INGREDIENTS
2 medium-sized truffles
30g/1oz butter
½ onion, finely chopped
1 thick rasher bacon, cut into
  strips
460g/1lb arborio rice
700ml/1¼ pints chicken stock
Salt and freshly ground black
  pepper

Preheat the oven to
200°C/400°F/Gas Mark 6. Using a
small, very sharp knife, cut the
truffles into thin slices. Heat the
butter gently in a large pan and
add the onion. Allow the onion
just to begin cooking, then stir in
the bacon and the rice, and cook
for 1 minute. Add the truffles and
the stock, season with salt and
pepper, then transfer to an
ovenproof dish. Cook, covered,
in the hot oven for
approximately 20 minutes. Serve
immediately.

RICE BALLS

These rich little mouthfuls of rice, meat and cheese require only a simple tossed salad for serving.

Serves 4

INGREDIENTS
200g/7oz arborio rice, cooked
120g/4oz minced beef
1 tsp freshly chopped parsley
60g/2oz Parmesan cheese
3 slices Mozzarella cheese
Salt and freshly ground black
  pepper
1 egg, beaten
Breadcrumbs
Oil for deep-frying

Mix together the rice and minced meat, then stir in the parsley, grated Parmesan and the Mozzarella, cut into small cubes. Season well with salt and pepper. Bind the mixture together using half of the beaten egg then, with slightly moist fingers, shape the mixture into small balls. Dip the rice balls in the remaining egg and then roll them in the breadcrumbs. Set the balls aside to rest for 20 minutes.

Heat the oil to 175°C/350°F and then lower in the rice balls. Fry until golden and crisp. Drain quickly on absorbent kitchen paper and serve as soon as possible.

109

INSALATA DI RISO ALLA ROMANA – RICE SALAD ROMAN STYLE

This salad is colourful and delicious – do take the time to wrap the anchovies around the olives for a special garnish.

Serves 6

INGREDIENTS
225g/½lb long-grain rice
120g/4oz uncooked cannellini beans, soaked overnight and drained
2 cloves garlic
½ tsp dried chilli flakes
45g/1½oz fresh white breadcrumbs, soaked in 90ml/ 3 fl oz beef stock and squeezed dry
150ml/¼ pint olive oil
3 tbsps red wine vinegar
1 tsp salt
120g/4oz diced lean prosciutto crudo
4 thick rashers bacon
60g/2oz can anchovy fillets, rinsed in cold water
8 large green olives
2 tbsps fresh basil leaves
2 tbsps marjoram

Cook the rice and beans separately in lightly salted water until tender. Drain and cool.

Grind the garlic and chilli flakes in a pestle and mortar. Add the squeezed breadcrumbs and beat in the oil, wine vinegar and salt.

Place the rice and beans in a salad bowl, and add the prosciutto. Cut the bacon into thin strips and cook in 1 tablespoon of oil until crisp. Drain the bacon and add it to the salad bowl. Stir in the bread sauce. Roll the anchovy fillets around the olives and arrange them on top of salad as decoration. Garnish with the basil and marjoram, roughly chopped into rather large pieces. Chill. Serve either as a luncheon dish or as antipasto.

RISOTTO ALLA MILANESE

This rich and delicious rice concoction is traditionally served with Osso Bucco. However, it is so delicious that I often serve it with a tossed green salad as a supper dish. It may be garnished with chopped parsley, grated lemon rind and freshly chopped garlic.

Serves 6-8

INGREDIENTS
120g/4oz butter
2 tbsps chopped beef marrow
½ small onion, chopped
Salt and freshly ground black
  pepper
150ml/¼ pint dry white wine
460g/1lb arborio rice
1 tsp saffron strands
1.14 litres/2 pints chicken stock
120g/4oz freshly grated
  Parmesan cheese

Melt half the butter in a saucepan, add the beef marrow, onion and a little salt and pepper. When the onion is soft but not brown, add the wine and let it boil and reduce to half its original volume. Stir in the rice. Dissolve the saffron in the stock and add it to the pan. Stir to keep the rice from sticking. Bring the stock to a simmer and shake the pan occasionally. Cook until the rice is *al dente* and the liquid is absorbed. Add more stock from time to time, if necessary, to prevent sticking. Stir in the remaining butter and grated Parmesan. Stand the pan over a very low heat for a few minutes, then serve.

111

VEGETABLE RISOTTO

*Risottos can be made from almost any selection of
ingredients, but they should always be moist and creamy.
This is quite a light risotto of vegetables. A welcome change
from heavy, rich food.*

Serves 4

INGREDIENTS
2 large leaves chard
60g/2oz butter
½ onion, finely chopped
1 carrot, diced
1 stick celery, diced
400g/14oz arborio rice, measured
   in a container
150g/5oz frozen peas
1 thick slice ham, diced
Salt and freshly ground black
   pepper

Preheat the oven to
200°C/400°F/Gas Mark 6. Cut the
green leaf part of the chard into
very thin strips and then cut the
white stalk into small dice. Heat
the butter in a large frying pan
and fry the onion, carrot, celery
and the green and white parts of
the chard for 2 minutes. Add the
rice, peas and ham, stir well and
cook until the rice is transparent.
Transfer to an ovenproof dish
and add water equivalent to 1½
times the volume of the
measured rice. Season with salt
and pepper and stir well. Cover
the dish and cook in a hot oven
for between 18 and 20 minutes.
Serve hot.

CHICKEN RISOTTO

A true risotto should be moist and creamy. Serve with a tossed green salad. This risotto is cooked in the oven, rather than on the hob.

Serves 4-6

INGREDIENTS
30g/1oz butter
1 white onion, cut into small dice
2 sticks celery, cut into small dice
1 carrot, cut into small dice
2 chicken legs, boned and the meat cut into small dice
460g/1lb arborio long-grain rice
Salt and freshly ground black pepper

Preheat the oven to 200°C/400°F/Gas Mark 6. Heat the butter in a casserole and gently fry the onion, celery and carrot for 2 minutes. Add the diced chicken, stir well and cook for 1 minute. Measure the rice in a container, then add it to the pan, stir well and cook until the rice is transparent. Add water to 3 times the volume of the rice used. Season with salt and pepper. Cover and cook in a hot oven for approximately 18 minutes until most of the liquid is absorbed. Serve hot.

RISI E BISI – RICE AND PEAS

I can remember learning to cook this in my very first job, to be served with a spicy lemon casserole. The proportions of peas and rice should be about equal.

Served 4-6

INGREDIENTS
90g/3oz bacon or prosciutto, as fat as possible
½ onion, chopped
60g/2oz butter
1 tbsp olive oil
460g/1lb fresh peas, hulled
Salt
1.14 litres/2 pints chicken stock
200g/7oz rice
60g/2oz Parmesan cheese
6 sprigs parsley, chopped

Sauté the chopped bacon and onion in half of the butter and the oil. When the onion is transparent, add the peas; salt lightly, stir and add the stock. Cover and cook over a moderate heat until the peas are half cooked. Add the rice and stir with a wooden spoon, taking care not to crush the peas, and complete cooking. The rice will take about 17 minutes to cook. Before removing from the heat, stir in the remaining butter, Parmesan and parsley. Stir again, stand for a few minutes, season and serve.

GNOCCHI WITH TOMATO SAUCE

Gnocchi, or Italian dumplings, make an excellent supper dish when served with a tomato sauce. They are crisped under a hot grill before serving – use Mozzarella rather than Parmesan over the gnocchi for a milder flavour.

Serves 4

INGREDIENTS
460g/1lb potatoes, steamed in their jackets
120g/4oz flour
1 egg yolk
120g/4oz Parmesan cheese, freshly grated
2 tbsps olive oil
1 shallot, finely chopped
1 clove garlic, chopped
6 tomatoes, peeled, seeded and roughly chopped
1 bouquet garni, made up with parsley, thyme and 1 bay leaf
Salt and freshly ground black pepper

Peel the potatoes and push them through a fine sieve. Beat the flour and egg yolk into the potato, then stir in 30g/1oz of the Parmesan cheese with salt and pepper. Place the gnocchi dough into a piping bag with a wide, straight nozzle.

Bring a large saucepan of salted water to the boil. Once the water is boiling, hold the bag over the pan and squeeze out balls of the dough, detaching the dough from the nozzle with the sharp downward movement of a knife. Remove the gnocchi from the pan with a slotted spoon as they rise to the surface and drain them on a cloth.

Heat the oil in a frying pan and gently fry the shallot and garlic, then add the tomatoes, bouquet garni, salt and pepper and simmer for approximately 15 minutes. The sauce should be quite liquid after this time. Remove the bouquet garni, place the sauce in a liquidiser or food processor and blend until smooth.

Return the sauce to the pan over a gentle heat, add the gnocchi and heat through. Tip into an ovenproof dish and top with the remaining Parmesan cheese. Crisp it under a hot grill and serve.

SPINACH GNOCCHI

Gnocchi are Italian dumplings. They should be light and are served plain as a starter, or with meat or a sauce as a main course.

Serves 4-6

INGREDIENTS
120g/4oz chopped, frozen
  spinach
225g/8oz Ricotta cheese
90g/3oz Parmesan cheese
Salt and freshly ground black
  pepper
Freshly grated nutmeg
1 egg, slightly beaten
45g/1½oz butter

Preheat the oven to 200°C/400°F/Gas Mark 6. Defrost the spinach and press it between two plates to extract all the moisture. Mix the spinach with the ricotta cheese, half the Parmesan, salt, pepper and nutmeg. Gradually add the egg, beating well until the mixture holds together when shaped. With floured hands, shape the mixture into ovals. Use about 1 tbsp mixture for each gnocchi.

Heat a pan of water until simmering. Lower the gnocchi into the water, 3 or 4 at a time, and allow them to cook gently until the gnocchi float to the surface in about 1-2 minutes. Remove with a slotted spoon and place in a well buttered ovenproof dish. When all the gnocchi are cooked, sprinkle with the remaining Parmesan cheese and dot with the remaining butter. Reheat for 10 minutes in the hot oven, then brown under a preheated grill before serving, if necessary.

PIZZA RUSTICA

This is a country pizza, almost more of a pie, made in a deep tin with lots of filling. If you can't find Fontina cheese use Edam or Gouda

Serves 4-6

INGREDIENTS
Pizza Dough
See recipe for Pizza with Peppers, Olives and Anchovies,

Filling
1 tbsp Parmesan cheese, grated
120g/4oz prosciutto or Parma ham, sliced
2 tomatoes, peeled, seeded and roughly chopped
60g/2oz Mozzarella cheese diced
1 tbsp freshly chopped parsley
1 tbsp freshly chopped basil
2 eggs, lightly beaten
5 tbsps double cream
60g/2oz Fontina cheese, finely grated
Pinch of nutmeg
Salt and freshly ground black pepper

Prepare the dough as for the Pizza with Peppers, Olives and Anchovies. When the dough has doubled in bulk, knock it back and knead lightly. Flatten the dough into a circle or rectangle and roll out to a circle about 25cm/10 inches in diameter or a rectangle about 28 × 18cm/11 × 7 inches. Lightly oil a baking tin, line it with the dough and press with floured fingertips to form a raised edge above sides of the tin.

Sprinkle the base of the dough with the Parmesan cheese then add a layer of ham. Cover the ham with the chopped tomato. Mix the remaining ingredients together and pour over the tomato and ham. Bake on the lowest shelf of the oven for about 35 minutes. The top of the pizza should be nicely browned and the edge of the dough should be golden when the pizza is ready. Serve hot.

WILD MUSHROOM PIZZA

*This pizza is made special by the use of wild mushrooms –
use a mixture of mushrooms if the wild varieties are not in
season – a few dried mushrooms will add extra flavour.*

Serves 4

INGREDIENTS
Bread Dough
250g/9oz strong plain flour, sifted
1 tbsp easy-blend yeast
Pinch of salt
120ml/4 fl oz tepid water
60ml/2 fl oz milk

Topping
60g/2oz butter
1 shallot, finely chopped
120g/4oz wild mushrooms, finely
  sliced
½ clove garlic, finely chopped
1 quantity tomato sauce (see
  Mozzarella Pizza)
4 button mushrooms, finely
  sliced
2 tbsps grated Parmesan cheese
20 olives
Salt and freshly ground black
  pepper

Place the flour, yeast and salt in a
large bowl, then add the liquids.
Mix to a manageable dough then
knead by hand for 3 minutes.
Cover with a cloth and leave to
rise in a warm place for 45
minutes.

Preheat the oven to
220°C/425°F/Gas Mark 7. Heat
the butter in a pan and fry the
shallot, mushrooms and garlic for
2 minutes. Roll out the dough on
a floured surface into the desired
thickness and shape – one large
or four small rounds. Transfer to
a baking sheet. Spread the
tomato sauce evenly over the
pizza dough, then place the
mushrooms on the sauce and
sprinkle with the grated
Parmesan cheese. Dot the olives
over the pizza and season with
salt and pepper. Cook in a very
hot oven until the dough base is
crisp and golden brown in 15-20
minutes. Serve immediately.

MOZZARELLA PIZZA

One of the best of the standard pizza recipes. This pizza can be dressed up with any topping of your choice.

Serves 4

INGREDIENTS

1 quantity bread dough (see Wild Mushroom Pizza)
2 tomatoes, sliced
½ onion, finely sliced
2 slices ham, cut into small pieces
200g/7oz Mozzarella cheese
Salt and freshly ground black pepper
1 tsp marjoram

Tomato Sauce

2 tbsps olive oil
1 onion, finely chopped
4 large tomatoes, seeded, skinned and crushed
1 bay leaf
1 small sprig thyme
A few drops of Tabasco sauce
1 clove garlic, finely chopped
Salt and freshly ground black pepper

Preheat the oven to 220°C/425°F/Gas Mark 7. To make the tomato sauce, heat the olive oil in a frying pan and fry the onion until soft but not brown. Then add the tomato, bay leaf, thyme, Tabasco and garlic. Season with salt and pepper and cook for approximately 30 minutes.

Stir frequently. Once the liquid from the tomatoes has almost evaporated, remove the bay leaf and the sprig of thyme. Allow the sauce to cool slightly and then blend in a liquidiser or food processor until smooth.

Roll the dough out into a round and transfer it to a baking sheet. Spread with the prepared tomato sauce, then lay the sliced tomato over the tomato sauce, and top with the onion and the ham. Cut the Mozzarella into thin slices and lay them over the pizza.

Season with salt, pepper and the marjoram. Cook in the preheated oven for about 15 minutes and serve immediately.

SOUFFLÉ PIZZA WITH CHEESE

This type of pizza is often called calzone, meaning folded, or a pocket. It looks like a Cornish pasty! I usually make 4 small pizzas, to be certain that everyone gets a fair share of dough and filling.

Serves 4

INGREDIENTS

1 quantity bread dough (see Wild Mushroom Pizza)
½ quantity tomato sauce (see Mozzarella Pizza)
1 large onion, chopped
2 small goat's cheeses, weighing 225g/8oz in total
Salt and freshly ground black pepper
1 tsp marjoram
1 tbsp olive oil
1 egg

Preheat the oven to 220°C/425°F/Gas Mark 7. Roll the dough out into a round on a lightly floured surface, then transfer it to a baking sheet. Pour the tomato sauce over half of the round and scatter the onion over. Break the cheese into small pieces and place over the onion, then season with salt and pepper and sprinkle with the marjoram and the olive oil. Beat the egg and brush over the edges of the dough. Fold one half of the round over the other half to form a half-moon shape. Press down well along the edges to seal. Cook in a very hot oven and remove when the pizza is lightly coloured on the surface, in about 20 minutes. Serve immediately.

SEAFOOD PIZZA

Some 'seafood' pizzas just have a little tuna to make them 'fishy'! This delicious pizza for a special occasion has plenty of cockles and mussels in the topping.

Serves 4

INGREDIENTS
225g/8oz cockles
460g/1lb mussels
120ml/4 fl oz white wine
1 quantity bread dough (see Wild Mushroom Pizza)
1 quantity tomato sauce (see Mozzarella Pizza)
1 large onion, finely sliced
2 cloves garlic, chopped
1 tsp freshly chopped marjoram
Salt and freshly ground black pepper
4 tbsps Parmesan cheese, chopped

Preheat the oven to 220°C/425°F/Gas Mark 7. Wash, brush and rinse the cockles and mussels well. Place them in a large saucepan with the white wine over a high heat. Shake the pan frequently until all the shells have opened. Set the pan aside to allow the contents to cool. Once the cockles and mussels are cooled, remove them from their shells, discarding any that have not opened.

Roll out the dough into a large round on a floured surface, then transfer it to a baking sheet. Pour the tomato sauce into the centre of the pizza, spreading it over the dough with the back of a tablespoon. Place the sliced onion over the tomato sauce, then the mussels and the cockles. Scatter with the garlic, and season with the marjoram, salt, pepper and Parmesan cheese. Cook in a very hot oven for approximately 15 to 25 minutes, depending on the thickness of the dough. Serve immediately.

GOAT'S CHEESE PIZZA

Goat's cheese has a slightly lactic flavour and makes a tasty pizza topping – I love it!

Serves 4

INGREDIENTS

1 quantity bread dough (see Wild Mushroom Pizza)
1 quantity tomato sauce (see Mozzarella Pizza)
1 onion, finely sliced
4 rashers bacon
2 goat's cheeses, about 225g/8oz in total
Salt and freshly ground black pepper
1 tbsp freshly chopped marjoram

Preheat the oven to 220°C/425°F/Gas Mark 7. Roll the dough out thinly into a large circle on a floured surface, and transfer to a baking sheet. Spread the tomato sauce over the dough and then sprinkle over the onion. Cut the bacon into small pieces and scatter over the pizza. Slice the goat's cheese with a finely serrated knife and lay the slices over the pizza, then season with salt and pepper, sprinkle with the marjoram and cook in a very hot oven for approximately 15 minutes. This pizza cooks quite quickly, as the dough is fairly thin.

INDIVIDUAL PIZZAS WITH EGG

*I love pizza toppings with egg – I always want mine cooked
'soft', so that it will run and blend with the other topping
ingredients.*

Serves 4

INGREDIENTS
1 quantity bread dough (see Wild
  Mushroom Pizza)
1 quantity tomato sauce (see
  Mozzarella Pizza)
1 large onion, finely sliced
4 rashers bacon, cut into small
  pieces
4 eggs
4 tbsps grated Parmesan cheese
Salt and freshly ground black
  pepper

Preheat the oven to
220°C/425°F/Gas Mark 7. Form
the dough into 4 equal pieces.
Roll each into a thin round on a
floured surface. Transfer the
bases to baking sheets. Spoon 5
tbsps of the tomato sauce over
each pizza base, spreading it
evenly over the dough. Scatter
the onion and then the bacon
evenly over the 4 pizzas, and
season with salt and pepper.
Break one egg over each pizza
and sprinkle with the grated
Parmesan. Cook in a very hot
oven for 10 to 15 minutes. Serve
immediately.

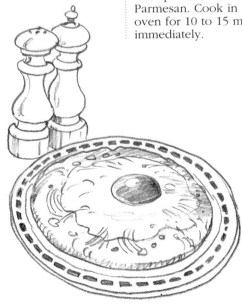

CRESPELLE ALLA BOLOGNESE

Crespelle.are Italian pancakes. There are many different ways of serving them, some of which reflect the regional flavour of Italian cookery. These are filled with a traditional Bolognese sauce.

Serves 6-8

INGREDIENTS

Bolognese Filling
30g/1oz butter or margarine
1 tbsp olive oil
2 onions, finely chopped
225g/8oz minced beef
1 small green pepper, seeded and finely chopped
120g/4oz canned plum tomatoes
1 tbsp tomato purée
150ml/¼ pint beef stock
1 bay leaf
2 tsps freshly chopped basil
1 tsp freshly chopped oregano
2 tbsps sherry
Salt and freshly ground black pepper

Crespelle Batter
3 eggs
120g/4oz plain flour
Pinch of salt
225g/8 fl oz water
2 tsps olive oil
Melted butter

Tomato Sauce
15g/½oz butter or margarine
1 clove garlic, crushed
1 onion, finely chopped
460g/1lb canned plum tomatoes
Salt and freshly ground black pepper
Fresh basil leaves

Heat the butter and oil in a deep saucepan for the Bolognese filling. Add the onion and cook slowly until soft but not coloured. Increase the heat and add the beef. Stir the beef while cooking until all the meat is browned. Add the chopped pepper, tomatoes and their juice, tomato purée, stock, herbs, salt and pepper to taste and simmer gently for about 45 minutes or until the mixture thickens, stirring occasionally. Add the sherry and cook for a further 5 minutes, then set aside.

Sift the flour for the crespelle with a pinch of salt. Break the eggs into a bowl and beat to mix thoroughly. Mix the eggs into the flour, beating all the time until the mixture is smooth. Add the water and oil and stir well. Cover the bowl with a damp cloth and leave in a cool place for 30 minutes.

Heat a crêpe pan or a 17.5cm/7 inch frying pan. Lightly grease with the melted butter and pour a large spoonful of the batter into the centre of the pan. Swirl the pan to coat the base evenly. Fry until the crespelle is brown on the underside, loosen the edge with a pallete knife, and turn over to brown the other side. Stack and wrap in a clean cloth until needed. Preheat the oven to 200°C/400°F/Gas Mark 6.

To make the tomato sauce, melt the butter in a small saucepan and cook the garlic and onion slowly for about 5 minutes, or until softened but not coloured. Reserve some whole basil leaves for garnish and chop a handful more. Add the tomatoes to the onions and garlic along with the chopped basil, salt, pepper and a pinch of sugar. Cook for about 10-15 minutes or until the onions are completely soft. Press the sauce through a sieve to remove the seeds, pressing the pulp against the sieve to extract as much liquid as possible.

To assemble, lay the crespelle out on a large, clean work surface and put 2 heaped spoonfuls of Bolognese filling into each. Roll up and place in an ovenproof dish. Repeat until all the crespelle have been filled.

Bake in the preheated oven for about 8 minutes. Heat the tomato sauce and spoon over the crespelle before serving. Garnish with basil leaves and serve immediately.

PRAWN CRESPELLE

A filling of prawns in a creamy white sauce is perfect for light Italian pancakes, served in a stack and sliced into portions to serve.

Serves 4

INGREDIENTS

To Make 12 Crespelle
90g/3oz flour
Pinch of salt
3 eggs
225ml/8 fl oz water
2 tsps olive oil
30g/1oz butter or margarine, melted

Filling
30g/1oz butter or margarine
15g/½oz flour
280ml/½ pint milk
Juice of 1 lemon
Salt and freshly ground black pepper
225g/8oz prawns, washed, peeled and de-veined

Garnish
1 lemon, cut into slices

First make the crespelle. Sift the flour with a pinch of salt. Break the eggs into a bowl and whisk. Add the flour gradually, whisking all the time until the mixture is smooth, then stir in the water and add the oil. Cover the bowl with a damp cloth and leave in a cool place for 30 minutes.

Preheat the oven to 200°C/400°F/ Gas Mark 6. Heat a crêpe pan or a 17.5cm/7 inch frying pan. Grease lightly with the melted butter and put a good tablespoon of batter in the centre. Tilt the pan to coat the surface evenly. Fry until the crespelle is brown on the underside, then loosen the edge with a palette knife; turn over and brown on the other side. Stack and wrap in a clean cloth until required.

To make the filling, heat the butter in a pan; stir in the flour, and cook for 1 minute. Remove from the heat and gradually stir in the milk. Return to the heat and bring to the boil, stirring all the time. Allow to simmer for 3 minutes. Stir in the lemon juice and salt and pepper to taste. Add half the sauce to the prawns. Place one crespelle in an ovenproof dish and add a spoon of prawn mixture. Cover with a crespelle and repeat, finishing with a crespelle on top. Bake in a preheated oven for 10 minutes. When ready to serve, cover with the remaining sauce. Garnish with lemon slices. Serve immediately.

SPINACH CRESPELLE

Crespelle are Italian pancakes and may be filled with countless stuffings. Spinach and nutmeg is, I think, a winning combination.

Serves 4

INGREDIENTS
12 crespelle
90g/3oz flour
Pinch of salt
3 eggs
225ml/8 fl oz water
2 tsps olive oil
30g/1oz butter or margarine,
  melted

Filling
225g/8oz packet frozen spinach,
  thawed
200g/7oz cream cheese
2 tbsps double cream
½ tsp grated nutmeg
Salt and freshly ground black
  pepper
60g/2oz Parmesan cheese, grated
30g/1oz butter or margarine

First make the crespelle. Sift the flour with a pinch of salt. Break the eggs into a bowl and whisk. Add the flour gradually, whisking all the time until the mixture is smooth, then stir in the water and add the oil. Cover the bowl with a damp cloth and leave in a cool place for 30 minutes. Heat a crêpe pan or a 17.5cm/7 inch frying pan. Grease lightly with the melted butter and put a good tablespoon of batter in the centre. Tilt the pan to coat the surface evenly. Fry until the crespelle is brown on the underside, then loosen the edge with a palette knife; turn over and brown on the other side. Stack and wrap in a clean cloth until required.

To make the filling, cook the spinach for 3 minutes in a pan of boiling water. Drain, chop and set aside. Beat the cream cheese and cream together until smooth, then add the nutmeg, half the Parmesan and salt and pepper to taste, and mix well. Stir the spinach into the cream cheese mixture. Divide equally between the 12 crespelle, placing the mixture at one end and rolling up. Place in an ovenproof dish and dot with butter. Sprinkle with Parmesan cheese and place under a hot grill for 5 minutes, or until lightly browned on top. Serve immediately.

FISH

Tuna – One of the Basic Ingredients of Italian Cooking

Tuna is popular throughout Italy and easy to obtain, being available in plentiful supply from Italian waters. I suppose it was a well-kept secret, a magic ingredient in authentic Italian cookery, until the canned tuna fish revolution took place, making it one of the most reasonable and versatile of ingredients in the modern store-cupboard. For preference I would always choose tuna canned in olive oil, but this is not always as easy to find as that in vegetable oil or brine.

Fresh tuna steaks are delicious but must be treated with care as they can be prone to dryness if they are cooked for too long. I always marinate the fish in a mixture of olive oil, lemon juice and herbs with just a touch of garlic, and then grill, pan-fry or

128

barbecue it very quickly, cooking it rare to keep it moist in the middle. Tuna is a meaty fish and is therefore quite filling, so don't be over-generous with the portions. Olive oil and seasonings were traditionally used in the home to preserve tuna fish after it had been boiled, making a delicious fish antipasti, but the wide availability of good canned tuna has led to a decline in this tradition.

Many fish benefit from being marinated before cooking and typical Italian herbs such as oregano and rosemary may be added to the marinade for extra flavour. Grilling is one of the most popular cooking methods for fish in Italy, and can scarcely be bettered if the fish is straight off the fishing boat and cooked on the beach.

Squid – a Personal Favourite

If the only time you tried squid you didn't like it, please do try it again! Most people's first experience is of deep fried rings of squid, quickly cooked in a fairly tasteless batter and then served with chips – this is not the best way to eat it, and I can well understand people being put off after just one bite.

In the recipe for Fried Squid the pieces are simply coated in flour before frying – they do not need a thick batter all over them. Squid may 'pop' during frying so do take care and keep a frying screen to hand if you have one. Although this is the best-known way of cooking squid, my preferences are for stuffing and steaming the whole squid, or for slicing and stewing them in a rich tomato sauce with plenty of garlic, red wine and some chilli pepper seasonings. If squid is cooked for an hour or more it becomes meltingly tender and looses any resemblance to rubber bands!

Sardines and Mussels – Simple Favourites for Sumptuous Feasts

Sardines are available throughout the Mediterranean waters and take their name from the island of Sardinia, the waters surrounding the island being a particularly good fishing ground for these versatile small fish. Like so many of the Mediterranean fish, sardines are really best grilled or shallow-fried. I have, however, included one recipe here for Stuffed Sardines, filled with spinach, capers and anchovies which make a typical Italian stuffing, bright and punchy in flavour and colourful in appearance. Boning sardines requires a little practice but they are so much nicer (and easier to eat) if all the bones are removed before cooking. I usually choose the largest sardines available and bone them like herrings, by pressing them flat on a chopping board and then easing the bones away.

The Venetians are also very keen on sardines and their classic regional recipe involves roasting the sardines quickly at a very high heat whilst basting them with a lemon marinade. They also eat plenty of eel and I have included a typical recipe for eel that is quickly fried and then finished in a red wine sauce.

The Italian waters yield a wonderful selection of seafoods including octopus, clams, lobsters and prawns and they also produce excellent mussels, one of my favourite seafoods. Mussels might seem complicated but, in reality, they are one of the simplest of foods to prepare. Clean them by rinsing and scraping off any encrustations from the shells and pulling off the beards, which are hairy threads that sometimes hang from the shells. The easiest way to cook mussels is by steaming them over white wine and seasonings but, if the meat is removed from the shells after cooking, the mussels may be added to sauces, rice or pasta. The recipe for Mussels Marinara makes a wonderful salad.

MUSSELS MARINARA

I always think of 'Marinara' as a pizza topping, but it is a tomato sauce which can be served with anything! Here it is made into a delicious mussel salad.

Serves 4

INGREDIENTS
1.14 litres/2 pints mussels
1 onion, chopped
120ml/4 fl oz white wine
Lemon juice
Salt and freshly ground black
  pepper
2 tbsps olive oil
1 clove garlic
1 shallot, chopped
680g/1½lbs tomatoes, chopped
1 tsp crushed oregano
1 bay leaf
1 tbsp freshly chopped basil
  leaves
1 tsp fennel seed
Pinch cayenne pepper

Garnish
Chopped parsley
Black olives

Scrub the mussels well, discarding any with broken shells. Place in a pan with the chopped onion, white wine, squeeze of lemon juice, salt and pepper. Cover and cook quickly until the mussels open, discarding any that do not. Remove the mussels from the shells and leave to cool.

Heat the olive oil in a saucepan and add the crushed garlic and shallot. Cook until just lightly brown. Blend in the tomatoes, herbs and fennel seeds. Add the seasoning and cooking liquid from the mussels and bring to the boil. Allow the sauce to boil rapidly until well reduced. Leave the sauce to cool, then mix with the mussels and chill. Serve garnished with the chopped parsley and black olives. Serve with a green salad and Italian bread

TUNA AND FENNEL

Fennel is sometimes referred to as Florence fennel. Always try to select a bulb with plenty of feathery green tops which are useful for garnish.

Serves 4

INGREDIENTS

1 clove garlic
4 tuna steaks, cut 2.5cm/1 inch thick
4 tbsps olive oil
4 tbsps white wine
Crushed black peppercorns
Salt
1 bulb fennel

Peel the garlic and cut into thin slivers. Insert these into the tuna steaks with a sharp knife. Mix together the oil, wine and crushed pepper then pour over the steaks in a shallow dish. Leave to marinate in the refrigerator for 1 hour.

Reserve the green, feathery tops of the fennel. Cut the head in half and slice into 6mm/¼ inch pieces. Cook in boiling salted water for 5 minutes. Heat the grill to high and grill the fish for 3-4 minutes per side, basting frequently with the marinade. Season the cooked fennel, drain and keep warm. Garnish the tuna steaks with the reserved fennel tops and serve with the cooked, sliced fennel.

FRITTO MISTO MARE

This is a cocktail of fish, coated in a lightly spiced batter and fried until golden and crisp. A real treat, and not too expensive as only small quantities of each fish are required.

Serves 4

INGREDIENTS
460g/1lb whitebait, smelts or sprats, or white fish such as sole or cod
225g/8oz uncooked scampi
120g/4oz scallops with roe attached
280ml/½ pint shelled mussels
Vegetable oil for deep-frying
Salt

Batter
2 tbsps olive oil
280ml/½ pint water
120g/4oz plain flour
Pinch of salt
1 tsp ground nutmeg
1 tsp ground oregano
1 egg white

Garnish
Parsley sprigs
1 lemon

First make the batter so that it can rest for 30 minutes while the fish is being prepared. Blend the oil and water, and gradually stir it into the flour sifted with a pinch of salt. Beat the batter until quite smooth, and add the nutmeg and oregano. Just before using, fold in the stiffly-beaten egg white.

If using smelts or sprats, cut the heads off the fish; if using white fish, cut into chunks about 2.5cm/1 inch thick. Shell the scampi if necessary. If the scallops are large, cut them in half. Heat the oil to 190°C/375°F. Dip fish and shellfish, one at a time, into the batter, allowing any surplus batter to drip off. Then put them into the frying basket and into the hot oil. Fry for 5-6 minutes, or until crisp and golden. Drain on crumpled absorbent kitchen paper. Sprinkle lightly with salt. Serve the fish on a heated serving dish and garnish with parsley sprigs and lemon wedges. If desired, a tartare sauce may be served.

MUSSELS ALLA GENOVESE

Mussels are quick and easy to cook. Leaving them in water with a little oatmeal or flour encourages them to clean themselves of any grit.

Serves 4

INGREDIENTS

1 litre/1¾ pints mussels
Flour or oatmeal
1 shallot, finely chopped
Lemon juice
Salt and freshly ground black pepper
1 handful fresh basil leaves
1 small bunch parsley
1 clove garlic
30g/1oz walnuts halves
2 tbsps freshly grated Parmesan cheese
30g/1oz butter
3-6 tbsps olive oil

Garnish

Fresh bay leaves or basil leaves

Scrub the mussels well and discard any with broken shells. Place in a bowl of clean water with a handful of flour or oatmeal. Leave for 30 minutes, then rinse under running water.

Place the chopped shallot in a large saucepan with the lemon juice. Cook until shallot softens. Add the mussels and a pinch of salt and pepper. Cover the pan and cook the mussels quickly, shaking the pan. When the mussel shells have opened, take the mussels out of the pan, set aside and keep warm. Strain the cooking liquor for possible use later.

To prepare the Genovese sauce, wash the basil leaves and parsley, peel the garlic clove and chop roughly, and chop the walnuts roughly. Put the herbs, garlic, nuts, 1 tbsp grated cheese and salt and pepper into a liquidiser or food processor and chop roughly. Add the butter and process again. Turn the machine on and add the oil gradually through the feed tube. If the sauce is still too thick, add the reserved liquid from the mussels. Remove the top shells from the mussels and discard. Arrange the mussels evenly in 4 shallow dishes, spoon some of the sauce into each, and sprinkle with the remaining Parmesan cheese. Garnish with bay or basil leaves and serve immediately.

KING PRAWN SALAD

Fresh prawns are now easily available in supermarkets and at fishmongers – they have a much better flavour than ready-cooked prawns.

Serves 4

INGREDIENTS
20 fresh king prawns
2 tbsps olive oil
1 carrot, finely sliced
½ onion, finely sliced
1 tbsp crushed tomato pulp or passata
½ bay leaf
1 tsp Cognac
1 tbsp double cream
60g/2oz butter
1 tsp sherry or wine vinegar
Salt and freshly ground black pepper
4 small servings fancy leaf lettuce

Peel and de-vein the prawns, discarding the heads, but retaining the peelings for the sauce. To make the sauce, heat 1 tbsp oil in a pan and fry the carrot, onion, tomato pulp, the peelings from the prawns and the ½ bay leaf. Fry for 2 minutes and then tip off the excess fat. Add the Cognac and cook until almost evaporated. Add water to cover the ingredients, and continue cooking, reducing the liquid until it is quite thick. Stir in the cream and bring the sauce to the boil. Strain through a very fine sieve, pressing the peelings to extract the juice.

Melt the butter in a frying pan and sauté the prawns for 2 minutes. Stir the vinegar into the sauce. Season with salt and pepper and then whisk in the remaining olive oil. Serve the prawns on a bed of washed, dried and chopped lettuce, with the sauce spooned over.

CALABRIAN OYSTERS

The ideal recipe for anyone put off oysters by the thought of eating them raw. These are cooked and seasoned in a typically Italian way with parsley and garlic.

Serves 4

INGREDIENTS

16 large oysters, opened
2 tbsps freshly chopped parsley
1 clove garlic, chopped
30g/1oz breadcrumbs
1 tbsp olive oil
Freshly ground black pepper

Preheat the oven to 200°C/400°F/Gas Mark 6. Using a small, sharp knife, remove the oysters from their shells. Place each oyster back into a half shell with a quarter of its original juice. Sprinkle a little parsley, garlic and breadcrumbs over each oyster. Add a few drops of olive oil and a sprinkling of freshly ground pepper. Place the oysters on a baking sheet and cook for 10 minutes in the oven. Serve immediately.

GRILLED TUNA
WITH ROSEMARY

Fresh tuna should be cooked slightly rare – overcooking will toughen the fish and make it dry.

Serves 4

INGREDIENTS
4 large tuna steaks
2 tbsps olive oil
1 tbsp freshly chopped parsley
1 tsp chopped rosemary
1 clove garlic, finely chopped
2 tbsps fresh breadcrumbs
Salt and freshly ground black
   pepper
2 lemons

Remove the bone from each tuna steak. Brush the steaks on one side with oil and sprinkle over half of the parsley, rosemary, garlic, breadcrumbs, salt and pepper. Preheat a cast iron griddle or a heavy frying pan.

When the griddle or frying pan is really hot, wipe over a little oil with a piece of absorbent kitchen paper and add the tuna steaks, herbed side down. Quickly brush the tops of the steaks with the remaining oil, and sprinkle with the remaining parsley, rosemary, garlic, breadcrumbs and a little salt and pepper. Turn the steaks to cook the other side.

Cook the tuna to your liking. If using a griddle, give the steaks a quarter turn on each side to give them a charred grid pattern. Serve immediately, accompanied by lemon halves.

STUFFED SARDINES

Anchovies, capers and spinach epitomise Italian cooking –
they certainly make my favourite pizza toppings! They also
make a tasty stuffing for sardines, which may be topped with
Parmesan cheese before baking.

Seryes 4

INGREDIENTS
4 anchovy fillets in oil
2 tsps capers
60g/2oz breadcrumbs
Salt and freshly ground black
  pepper
120g/4oz spinach, cut into strips
1 egg
1 tbsp onion, finely chopped
1 tbsp freshly chopped parsley
12 sardines, washed, gutted and
  boned
2 tbsps olive oil

Preheat the oven to
180°C/350°F/Gas Mark 4. Chop
the anchovies and the capers
together, then stir in the
breadcrumbs and a little salt and
pepper.

Mix the spinach with the egg,
onion and parsley, and add to
the stuffing mixture. Stir well to
mix the ingredients thoroughly.
Fill each of the sardines with the
stuffing and place them upright
in an ovenproof dish. Drizzle
with the olive oil and cook in the
oven for approximately 15
minutes. Serve hot.

WHELK AND COCKLE SALAD

A sophisticated salad of seaside treasure trove. Buy the whelks and cockles ready prepared if you prefer.

Serves 4

INGREDIENTS
32 large whelks
300g/11oz cockles
1 carrot, sliced
1 leek, sliced
1 onion, sliced
175ml/6 fl oz white wine
1 sprig thyme
1 bay leaf
Small bunch chives
Juice of 1 lemon
2 fl oz olive oil
Salt and freshly ground black pepper
4 small servings of mixed fancy leaf lettuce, washed and dried

Wash the shellfish really well in lots of cold water. Brush the shells with a small nail brush to remove any sand or grit. Change the water frequently, or rinse under cold, running water once you think they are clean.

Place the whelks in a saucepan of water with the carrot, leek and onion. Bring to the boil and then simmer gently for approximately 2 hours, until cooked. Cooking time will depend on the size of the whelks.

Place the cockles in a frying pan with the white wine, thyme and bay leaf. Cover, bring to a brisk boil and cook until the shells open. Remove from the heat when the shells have opened and allow to cool. Once they are cool enough to handle, remove the cockles from their shells and discard everything else.

When the whelks are cooked, set them aside to cool and then remove them from their shells. Pull off any black parts from the body of the whelk and also the muscle at the bottom of the body. The intestinal tract may also be removed, if desired.

Chop the chives finely and stir them into the lemon juice, olive oil, salt and pepper. Toss the prepared lettuce, whelks and cockles in the sauce and serve on small individual plates.

EEL IN RED WINE

Eel is a rich, meaty fish. This recipe, which is impressive but quick to prepare, prepares the eel in a rich wine and tomato sauce.

Serves 4

INGREDIENTS
570g/1¼lbs eel, skinned
Salt and freshly ground black
  pepper
2 tbsps olive oil
2 onions, finely sliced
1 clove garlic, chopped
300ml/11 fl oz red wine
1 tsp sugar
3 tbsps crushed tomato pulp
120ml/4 fl oz fish stock

Preheat the oven to 180°C/350°F/Gas Mark 4. Cut the eel into medium-thick slices and season with salt and pepper. Heat the oil in a large pan and fry the onion and garlic for 1 minute. Add the eel slices to the pan and seal on both sides. Stir the wine and sugar into the pan, cook until the wine reduces slightly, then add the tomato and the fish stock. Season with salt and pepper. Transfer to an ovenproof dish and finish cooking in the preheated oven for 15 minutes.

Remove the eel from the dish and, if the sauce is not very thick, pour it into a saucepan and reduce it over a high heat to thicken. Serve the eel hot, with the sauce poured over.

RED MULLET WITH
VINAIGRETTE SAUCE

Ask your fishmonger to fillet the red mullet for you – it is quite a fiddly job and requires a very sharp knife. Use sherry vinegar for this recipe if you can – it has the most wonderful flavour.

Serves 4

INGREDIENTS

60ml/2oz sherry or wine vinegar
10 leaves fresh basil, cut into thin
   strips
Salt and freshly ground black
   pepper
120ml/4 fl oz olive oil
2 tomatoes, seeded and diced
2 tbsps oil
6 red mullet, emptied, scaled and
   filleted

Mix together the vinegar, basil, salt, pepper and the olive oil. Stir in the diced tomato once the sauce is well mixed.

In a frying pan, heat the oil and fry the fish fillets, skin side first. When fried on both sides, remove and drain on absorbent kitchen paper. Place the fried fillets in a bowl, pour over the sauce and leave to marinate for at least 1 hour before serving.

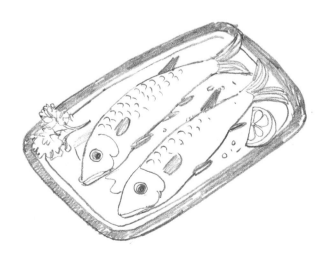

STUFFED SQUID

*I adore squid! They are not difficult to·stuff – the best way is
to use a forcing bag with a large plain nozzle for the filling.
These squid are served with a lemon vinaigrette.*

Serves 4

INGREDIENTS
250g/9oz white fish fillets,
  skinned
1 egg
4 anchovy fillets in oil
2 tbsps single cream
Salt and freshly ground black
  pepper
8 medium squid, cleaned and
  washed
1 tbsp double cream
1 tbsp lemon juice
2 tbsps olive oil
1 lettuce, washed, dried and
  broken into small pieces
2 tomatoes, sliced or cubed

Place the fish, egg, anchovies,
single cream, salt and pepper in
a liquidiser or food processor
and blend until smooth. Place in
the refrigerator for 30 minutes.

Cook the squid in a steamer for
10 minutes. When cooked, rinse
in cold water and set aside to
drain. Press the fish mixture
through a fine sieve, pushing it
through with the back of a
spoon. Using a spatula, mix the
double cream into the fish
stuffing. Fill the squid with the
fish stuffing and then tie up the
ends using a needle and thread.
Place the stuffed squid in a
steamer and cook for 15 minutes.

Mix together the lemon juice,
olive oil, salt and pepper and
toss the lettuce in the dressing.
Place a little salad on 4 plates,
add the tomato and serve with
the stuffed squid, either hot or
cold, sliced into rounds.

142

MARINATED SARDINES

This is a typically Italian way of cooking sardines – in wine vinegar with pine nuts. The sardines are cooked and then left to marinate for one or two days.

Serves 4

INGREDIENTS
20 evenly-sized sardines
Flour for dredging
Salt and freshly ground black
 pepper
3-4 tbsps oil
1 tbsp olive oil
2 large onions, finely sliced
45g/1½oz pine nuts
200ml/7 fl oz wine vinegar

Remove the heads from the sardines, then gut and bone the fish. Dredge the fillets in the flour and season with plenty of salt and pepper. Heat the cooking oil in a frying pan, and fry the fillets on both sides, then drain on absorbent kitchen paper.

Heat the olive oil in a frying pan and gently fry the onions and pine nuts for a few minutes. Add the vinegar to the pan and continue cooking for 30 seconds. Remove from the heat and set aside to cool slightly. Place the sardines in a large dish, putting a little of the onion mixture between each fillet. Pour the warm vinegar over the sardines and leave to marinate in a cool place for a few days.

SGOMBRO RIPIENO –
HERB STUFFED MACKEREL

*Mackerel are oily fish with plenty of flavour. This simple
stuffing of onions and herbs complements the fish well.*

Serves 1

INGREDIENTS
1 medium mackerel
1 small sprig rosemary
1 tsp freshly chopped thyme
3 tbsps freshly chopped parsley
1 tsp finely chopped onion
2 tbsps white wine
1 tbsp olive oil
Salt and freshly ground black
  pepper

Preheat the oven to
180°C/350°F/Gas Mark 4. Clean
the fish but leave the head and
tail on. Stuff the body of the
mackerel with the rosemary,
thyme, parsley and onion. Lay
the fish in a shallow baking tin
and pour over the white wine
and olive oil. Sprinkle with salt
and pepper. Bake, uncovered,
for 20-25 minutes. Garnish with
more fresh sprigs of rosemary
and thyme.

PESCE AL MARSALA – FISH WITH MARSALA

One of the secrets of cooking prime ingredients is to keep the recipe simple. The sole in Italy is of luxurious quality and requires very little adornment.

Served 3-4

INGREDIENTS
460g/1lb sole fillets
1 small onion
Seasoned flour
2 tbsps oil for frying
4 tbsps Marsala
1 lemon
Salt and white pepper

Skin the sole. Boil the skins with the sliced onion for 15 minutes in a little water to make 4-5 tbsps stock. Lightly flour the fish fillets. Heat the oil in a large frying pan, add the fish and sauté the fillets on both sides until golden. Add the Marsala and the strained fish stock. Cook gently for a further 10 minutes.

Cut the lemon in two and squeeze the juice of one half on to the fish, then season with salt and pepper. Place the fish fillets on a warmed serving platter. Pour the pan juices over and garnish with the remaining half lemon cut into slices.

SALMON TROUT WITH GARLIC SAUCE

Salmon trout is only in season for a matter of weeks, so make this dish whenever you have the opportunity. Serve with a tossed green salad.

Serves 4

INGREDIENTS
Court Bouillon
200ml/8 fl oz water
200ml/8 fl oz dry white wine
1 carrot, chopped
1 stick celery, chopped
1 sprig parsley, chopped
1 small onion, chopped
Salt
4 peppercorns
Juice of ½ lemon

900g/2lb salmon trout, cleaned
   with head and tail left on
460g/1lb potatoes, peeled and
   diced
4 cloves garlic, chopped
90g/3oz fresh breadcrumbs
2 tbsps wine vinegar
Freshly ground black pepper
7 tbsps olive oil
2 lemons
60g/2oz melted butter

Combine all the ingredients for the court bouillon, bring to the boil and simmer for 5 minutes. Place the trout in a fish kettle, or large pan and cover with court bouillon. Bring to the boil, then simmer for 12 minutes.

Boil the potatoes in salted water until tender. Grind the garlic in a mortar, add the bread soaked in vinegar, salt and pepper. Add the oil, drop by drop and beat until smooth. Drain the trout and transfer to a serving platter. Garnish with lemon halves and surround it with boiled potatoes mixed with melted butter. Spoon the garlic sauce over the salmon trout and serve.

CALAMARETTI ALLA BARESE – SQUID BARI STYLE

The Italians have really worked out how to cook squid! In recipes such as this, where it is cooked slowly for an hour or more, the squid becomes meltingly tender and looses all chewiness.

Serves 6

INGREDIENTS
900g/2lbs small squid
2 cloves garlic, chopped
175ml/6 fl oz olive oil
460ml/16 fl oz passata
Salt and freshly ground black
  pepper
6 sprigs parsley, chopped

Clean the squid. Wash them repeatedly in cold running water and separate the sac and tentacles. Sauté the garlic in 7 tbsps of the olive oil, then add the passata. Season with salt and pepper and simmer the sauce for about 10 minutes. In another pan, sauté the squid in the remaining oil, turning constantly. Pour the sauce over the squid and simmer, covered, for 1 hour or until the squid are tender. Sprinkle chopped parsley over the dish and serve.

FISH STEW

Various combinatiuons of seafood may be used in fish stews, but try this one for a deliciously authentic taste of Italy.

Serves 4

INGREDIENTS

1 medium mackerel, cleaned
225g/8oz halibut
2 lemon sole fillets
4 tbsps olive oil
1 medium onion, sliced
2 cloves garlic, chopped
2 tbsps freshly chopped parsley
1 bay leaf
½ cucumber, diced
225g/½lb tomatoes, skinned, seeded and chopped
4 tbsps white wine
280ml/½ pint water
4 slices ciabata or other Italian bread
Salt and freshly ground black pepper and sugar
225g/8oz scampi, cooked, shelled and de-veined

Skin and fillet the mackerel, discarding the head and tail. Cut into thin, bite-sized slices. Cut the halibut into bite-sized pieces, and the sole into 2.5cm/1 inch strips. Heat the oil in a large frying pan and sauté the sliced onion and garlic for 2-3 minutes. Add the parsley, bay leaf, diced cucumber, and chopped tomatoes. Sauté for 1-2 minutes then add the wine, water and seasoning. Cover and simmer gently for 20 minutes.

Preheat the oven to 180°C/350°F/Gas Mark 4. Add the fish except the scampi to the stew, with a little more water if necessary. Cover and simmer for a further 10 minutes. Add the scampi for the last 5 minutes. Meanwhile, rub the bread with a cut piece of garlic and bake in the oven. Place one slice in the base of each serving plate then spoon the stew over. Garnish with more chopped parsley before serving.

BARBECUED WHITING
SARDINIAN STYLE

Bay leaves have a wonderful flavour, which is especially good with fish. I prefer to use dried bay leaves as they have a better flavour, but fresh leaves could be used.

Serves 4

INGREDIENTS
2 whitings weighing about
   1.15kg/2½lbs in total
Bay leaves
Salt and freshly ground black
   pepper
Olive oil

Clean the whiting, discard the heads and cut each fish into 4 thick slices. Spear the pieces on heatproof skewers, alternating whiting with bay leaves. Season with salt, pepper and brush with oil. Cook, 6 inches above grey charcoal, basting as necessary with oil until the fish is cooked; this will take about 10 to 15 minutes.

FRESH SARDINES
LIGURIAN STYLE

The fresh sardines are boned, stuffed and shallow-fried. The cheesy, herbed stuffing complements the flavour of the fish perfectly.

Serves 4

INGREDIENTS
16 fresh sardines
10g/scant ½oz dried mushrooms, soaked and chopped
Olive oil
Salt and freshly ground black pepper
4 slices stale white bread
Milk
1 tbsp freshly grated Parmesan cheese
1 clove garlic, chopped
Several sprigs fresh marjoram
1 tbsp freshly chopped oregano
3 eggs
Plain flour
Dry breadcrumbs

Clean the sardines, discarding the heads and tails. Slit them open on one side but without separating the halves. Carefully remove the bones.

Sauté the mushrooms in 2 tablespoons of oil. Sprinkle with a little salt and place them in a bowl. Soak the stale bread in milk. Squeeze it out well, then add it to the mushrooms with the Parmesan, garlic, marjoram, oregano, 1 egg and a pinch of salt. Mix well. Place a little of the mixture into each sardine. Coat the sardines with flour then dip them into the remaining beaten eggs and then into the breadcrumbs, pressing the crumbs firmly onto the fish. Fry in hot oil until brown on both sides. Serve piping hot.

SOLE WITH PINE NUTS

Pine nuts are used extensively in Italian cookery – they are sweetly flavoured and make an attractive garnish for many dishes.

Serves 4

INGREDIENTS
8 fillets of sole, skinned
Plain flour
2 tbsps olive oil
120g/4oz butter
150ml/¼ pint white wine vinegar
150ml/¼ pint water
225g/8oz white grapes, halved
  and pipped
2 tbsps pine nuts
Salt and freshly ground black
  pepper

Coat the fish fillets lightly in flour. Heat the oil and butter in a large frying pan, and sauté the fish gently until golden brown on both sides. Add more oil or butter if necessary. Place the fillets on a serving dish and keep warm.

Add the white wine vinegar to the frying pan with the water, grapes and pine kernels; season, and simmer gently for 5-7 minutes, until the liquid has almost evaporated. Pour the contents of the pan over the fish and serve.

TUSCAN-STYLE
RED MULLET

This red mullet dish is just as good hot or cold. Red mullet has a meaty, gamey flavour and copes well with this robust treatment.

Serves 4

INGREDIENTS
4 tbsps olive oil
1 shallot, chopped
½ onion, finely chopped
1 clove garlic, chopped
6 large tomatoes, peeled, seeded and roughly chopped
1 tsp freshly chopped parsley
½ tsp marjoram
1 tsp sugar
Salt and freshly ground black pepper
1 tbsp wine vinegar
8 small red mullet, gutted, scaled and cut into fillets

Heat 2 tbsps of olive oil in a frying pan and gently fry the shallot, onion, garlic and tomato. Stir well and cook for 2 minutes. Stir in the parsley, marjoram, sugar, salt and pepper. Cook for 30 minutes over a very low heat. Add the vinegar and blend until smooth in a liquidiser or food processor. Season to taste

Heat the remaining oil in a frying pan, and fry the red mullet fillets, skin side down first, and then pat them dry with absorbent kitchen paper. Serve the fillets hot, warm or cold, with the sauce poured over.

FRIED SCAMPI

Frozen prepared scampi is one thing – freshly prepared scampi cooked at home is quite different.

Serves 4

INGREDIENTS
20 small scampi
Salt and freshly ground black
  pepper
Oil for deep-frying
Flour for dredging
1 egg yolk
½ tsp mustard
5 fresh basil leaves, finely
  chopped
200ml/7 fl oz olive oil
1 clove garlic, finely chopped
1 lemon
1 egg

Remove the heads and peel the scampi. Season with salt and pepper and then dredge them in the flour. Shake to remove excess flour.

Beat together the egg yolk, mustard, some salt and pepper and the fresh basil. Add the olive oil in a thin, steady trickle, whisking continuously until a thick mayonnaise is obtained. Stir the finely chopped garlic into the mayonnaise. Peel the lemon, separate the segments and remove the membrane. Cut the flesh into tiny pieces and set aside.

Heat the oil to 175°C/350°F. Beat the egg and briefly dip the scampi into it. Place the scampi in the hot oil and fry until crisp and golden. Drain on absorbent kitchen paper and serve with a little lemon and the mayonnaise.

SPRATS IN MAYONNAISE

Sprats are tiny herrings and are at their best during the winter months. Serve the sprats on a bed of mixed salad leaves.

Serves 4

INGREDIENTS
1 carrot
1 sprig rosemary
Small bunch parsley
1 bay leaf
Salt and freshly ground pepper
570g/1¼lbs sprats
1 egg yolk
1 tsp mustard
1 clove garlic, chopped
120ml/4 fl oz olive oil

Make a vegetable stock by adding the carrot, rosemary, parsley and bay leaf to a large pan of water. Season well with salt and pepper and simmer gently until the liquid is well flavoured. Strain the stock into a clean saucepan through a fine sieve. Bring the stock to a gentle simmer and add the fish. Cook for approximately 2 minutes (longer if you prefer your fish very well done). Drain and set the fish aside to cool.

To make the mayonnaise, beat together the egg yolk, mustard, salt, pepper and garlic, then add the olive oil drop by drop, beating continuously. Serve the fish hot or cold with the mayonnaise.

FISH MILANESE

Any Italian dish cooked 'Milanese' is flavoured with lemons.
In this recipe fillets of white fish have a crispy crumb coating
and a tangy lemon dressing.

Serves 4

INGREDIENTS

8 sole or plaice fillets, skinned
2 tbsps dry vermouth
1 bay leaf
6 tbsps olive oil
Salt and freshly ground black
  pepper
Seasoned flour for dredging
2 eggs, lightly beaten
Dry breadcrumbs
Oil for shallow-frying
90g/3oz butter
1 clove garlic, crushed
2 tsps chopped parsley
2 tbsps capers
1 tsp freshly chopped oregano
Juice of 1 lemon
Lemon wedges and parsley to
  garnish

Skin the fillets with a sharp filleting knife. Remove any small bones and place the fillets in a large, shallow dish. Combine the vermouth, bay leaf and oil in a small saucepan and heat gently. Allow to cool completely then pour over the fish. Leave the fish to marinate for about 1 hour, turning the fillets occasionally.

Remove the fish from the marinade and dredge it lightly with the seasoned flour. Dip the fillets into the beaten eggs to coat them, or use a pastry brush to brush the eggs onto the fillets. Dip the egg-coated fish into the breadcrumbs, pressing the crumbs on firmly.

Heat the oil in a large frying pan. Add the fillets and cook slowly on both sides until golden brown. Cook for about 3 minutes on each side. Remove the fillets and drain on absorbent kitchen paper. Pour the oil out of the frying pan and wipe it clean. Add the butter and the garlic and cook until both turn a light brown. Add the herbs, capers and lemon juice and pour immediately over the fish. Garnish with lemon wedges and sprigs of parsley.

RED MULLET WITH HERB AND MUSHROOM SAUCE

Red mullet is popular throughout the Mediterranean – it is a meaty fish which can take robust seasonings. Cook the mullet with its liver left inside.

Serves 4

INGREDIENTS
460g/1lb small mushrooms, left whole
1 clove garlic, finely chopped
3 tbsps olive oil
Juice of 1 lemon
1 tbsp freshly chopped parsley
2 tsps freshly chopped basil
1 tsp chopped marjoram or sage
4 tbsps dry white wine mixed with ½ tsp cornflour
Few drops anchovy essence
4 red mullet, each weighing about 225g/8oz
2 tsps white breadcrumbs
2 tsps freshly grated Parmesan cheese

Preheat the oven to 190°C/375°F/Gas Mark 5. Combine the mushrooms, garlic and olive oil in a small frying pan. Cook over a moderate heat for about 1 minute, until the garlic and mushrooms are slightly softened. Add all the herbs, lemon juice and the white wine and cornflour mixture. Bring to the boil and cook until thickened. Add anchovy essence to taste, then set aside while preparing the fish.

To clean the fish, cut along the stomach from the gills to the vent, the small hole near the tail. Clean out the cavity of the fish, leaving the liver, if desired. To remove the gills, lift the flap and snip them out with a sharp pair of scissors. Rinse the fish well and pat dry. Place the fish head to heal in a shallow ovenproof dish that can be used for serving. The fish should fit snugly into the dish. Pour the prepared sauce over the fish and sprinkle with the breadcrumbs and Parmesan cheese. Cover the dish loosely with foil and cook in the preheated oven for about 20 minutes. Uncover for the last 5 minutes, if desired, and raise the oven temperature slightly. This will lightly brown the fish.

156

SWORDFISH KEBABS

Swordfish is ideal for kebabs as it will not fall apart during cooking. It is a popular fish throughout Italy, but especially in the south and in Sicily. These kebabs also cook well on a barbecue.

Serves 4-6

INGREDIENTS
1kg/2¼lbs swordfish steaks
90ml/3 fl oz olive oil
1 tsp freshly chopped oregano
1 tsp freshly chopped marjoram
Juice and rind of ½ a lemon
4 tomatoes, cut in thick slices
2 lemons, cut in thin slices
Salt and freshly ground black
    pepper
Lemon slices and Italian parsley
    for garnish

Cut the swordfish steaks into 5cm/2 inch pieces. Mix the olive oil, herbs, lemon juice and rind together and set it aside. Thread the swordfish, tomato slices and lemon slices on skewers, alternating the ingredients. Brush the skewers with the oil and lemon juice mixture and cook under a preheated grill for about 10 minutes, basting frequently with the lemon and oil. Serve garnished with lemons and parsley.

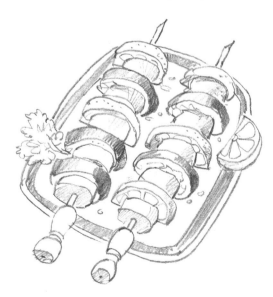

DEVILLED LOBSTER ITALIAN STYLE

A delicious way of serving lobster. Use ready-cooked lobsters if you prefer, although the flavour is always better if you cook them yourself. The coral and the liver of the lobster are mixed into the mustard sauce.

Serves 2 as a main course or 4 as a starter

INGREDIENTS
2 live lobsters, about 680/1½lbs each
45g/1½oz butter
1 tbsp Dijon or Italian mustard
60ml/2 fl oz brandy
Salt and freshly ground black pepper
2 tbsps olive oil
3 tbsps dry breadcrumbs
2 lemons sliced

Drop the lobsters into boiling salted water. Return to the boil, then cook for 5 minutes. Drain and drench with cold water. Cut the lobsters in half lengthways, and crack the legs and claws. Remove the "sand sack" and dark coloured intestine. Reserve the coral and tomalley, the green coloured liver.

Preheat the oven to 190°C/375°F/Gas Mark 5. Beat the butter until it is creamy. Stir in the mustard and creamy parts of the lobster after pressing them through a sieve. Warm the brandy, ignite it then pour it, flaming, over the mixture. When the flames subside, sprinkle with salt and pepper and mix thoroughly.

Brush a baking dish with oil. Place the lobster halves on the baking sheet, cut side up. Spread some of the mustard sauce over them. Bake in the preheated oven for about 15 minutes, basting from time to time with pan juices. Meanwhile mix the breadcrumbs with the remaining mustard sauce. Remove the baking sheet from the oven and spread the mixture over the lobster halves. Bake for a further 5 minutes until well-browned. Place on a serving platter with shredded lettuce and lemon slices. Pour the pan juices over and serve.

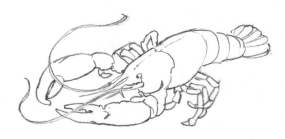

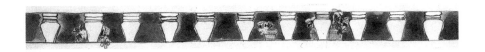

CALAMARETTI FRITTI –
FRIED SQUID

Frying is the most popular method of serving squid, although the Italians also make wonderful squid stews. This is a quick and easy dish to prepare.

Serves 4-6

INGREDIENTS
900g/2lbs small squid
Plain flour
Oil for frying
Salt
2 lemons cut in halves

Clean the squid. Wash in cold running water and separate sac and tentacles. Cut into bite-sized pieces and coat lightly with flour.

Heat some oil in a deep fryer to 185°C/360°F. Deep-fry the squid until golden brown. Season with salt, arrange on a serving platter and garnish with lemon halves.

CRISP-FRIED SPRATS

*Sprats are tiny herrings, often found in Mediterranean
waters. The more simply they are cooked the better, I think,
they are. Serve with lemon mayonnaise.*

Serves 4

INGREDIENTS
570g/1¼lbs sprats
Oil for deep-frying
150g/5oz flour
2 lemons
Salt and freshly ground black
    pepper

Wash the sprats well in plenty of
cold water, then dry them on a
cloth. The fish must be
completely dry.

Heat the oil to 175°C/350°F. Toss
the fish in the flour and then
shake off any excess. Lower the
fish into the hot oil, and fry until
crisp and golden. Drain on
absorbent paper and serve with
lemon rounds, salt and pepper.

OCTOPUS AND SQUID SALAD

This, for me, is Italian cooking at its best – a delicious salad of octopus and squid!

Serves 4

INGREDIENTS
340g/12oz squid
340g/12oz octopus
2 tbsps lemon juice
2 tbsps olive oil
Salt and freshly ground black
   pepper
½ tsp chopped marjoram
1 clove garlic, chopped
1 tsp freshly chopped parsley
1 large lettuce

Prepare and wash the squid and the octopus. Cook them in boiling water for approximately 30 minutes, or until cooked through and reasonably tender, then rinse under cold water and set aside to drain. Once well drained, cut them into thin rounds and then into small dice.

Mix together the lemon juice, olive oil, salt, pepper, marjoram, garlic and the parsley. Mix the squid and octopus into the sauce and leave to marinate for a few hours. Wash the lettuce, break the leaves into bite-sized pieces and place on 4 individual plates. Serve the prepared octopus and squid on the bed of lettuce with the marinade poured over.

CHICKEN & VEAL

The Ever-Popular Chicken

Just about every cuisine that I have explored has featured chicken in a big way. It is such a versatile ingredient, light in its own flavour and readily accepting of those of other foods and seasonings cooked with it. It can be fired up with chillis for a spicy dish to warm you through on the coldest of winter days, or served in a creamy sauce flavoured delicately with saffron and nestling in a bed of rice, for a light dish to tempt the most conservative of eaters.

Chickens are also part of the classic cuisine of most countries because they are highly skilled at scavenging and fending for themselves in the country, where they can be contained in large pens and virtually left to themselves. They have always been important on small farms as they give eggs for many months before they are ready for the pot. I cannot think of a single national cuisine that doesn't feature chicken recipes, often evolved from simple country dishes. Italy is no exception. Combine chicken with tomatoes, one of the best-known of Italian ingredients, and you have the basis of many fine meals. The simple recipe for Chicken with Tomato Sauce sets the scene, and can easily be developed into Chicken Cacciatore, hunter's chicken, with mushrooms, garlic and olives, and vermouth in the tomato sauce.

Chicken meat is one of the most versatile of ingredients – of course it is delicious simply roasted, or marinated in olive oil, lemon juice and oregano, in typical Italian style, and then grilled. Most of the recipes in this chapter are for casseroles or dishes where the chicken is the main ingredient but it is, of course, widely used in other dishes such as risottos and pasta sauces. Only a small amount of chicken can add a great deal of flavour to such dishes – there is an excellent recipe for Chicken Risotto in the chapter on rice cookery.

A Humane Approach to Veal Farming

Veal is just as popular as chicken, if not more so, in Italy. Veal is the meat of a young cow, a calf, and has been enjoyed for as long as beef. Beef cattle have descended from the first wild oxen to be domesticated some 8,000 years ago by the earliest farmers in Macedonia.

The very best veal tends to be milk fed, often intensively, to yield a heavier veal calf whilst retaining the milky pinkness of the young flesh and its fine, lightly grained texture. Such calves are slaughtered at four or five months old and France, Holland and the UK produce most of their veal in this way, often leading to criticism by all except gourmets of the production methods of the meat. In Italy, however, the veal is not usually intensively fed on milk and the flesh is consequently redder in colour, with a slightly more pronounced flavour. This more humane and less intensive production may well explain the popularity of the meat in the Italian cuisine.

Osso Buco – a True Italian Classic

Probably the best known of all Italian veal recipes is Osso Buco, a delicious casserole of shin of veal in a tomato sauce. The meat is cut into thick slices, one per helping, across the veal shin, leading to the cut often being referred to as osso buco rather than shin. There is plenty of marrow in the bone which adds greatly to the flavour and consistency of the sauce. I have included two recipes for Osso Buco in this chapter, one in the classic Milanese style and one a contemporary recipe where almond flavoured marsala is added to the sauce in place of wine. Shin of veal is sometimes referred to as 'veal birds' in America, where cuts of meat are often given different names to those used in Europe. The recipe for Skewered Veal Birds does not refer to this cut of veal, but to mixed meat kebabs.

Many classic veal recipes call for scaloppines of veal, but very few butchers actually cut these correctly. They have to come from the top of the topside and be cut across the grain of the meat. That, however, is only the start of the matter as the meat then has to be pounded until thin and even. If buying escalopes or scaloppines of veal from a cold cabinet do not buy those where you can see the grain running with the slice of the meat – they will never really cook tender and will therefore produce a disappointing finished dish.

CHICKEN WITH TOMATO SAUCE

I wonder how many litres of tomato sauce are consumed in Italy each year! In this recipe the versatile sauce is cooked with chicken joints.

Serves 4

INGREDIENTS
1 large chicken
280ml/½ pint red wine
2 tbsps oil
1 onion, chopped
280ml/½ pint tomato juice
2 rasher bacon, chopped into
  small pieces
280ml/½ pint chicken stock
1 sprig tarragon
12 baby onions
Salt and freshly ground black
  pepper

Joint the chicken into 2 leg and 2 breast portions, retaining the carcase and wings for stock. In a saucepan, bring the red wine to the boil and then ignite; this helps to remove the acidity of the wine. Remove from the heat. Heat the oil in a frying pan and brown the chicken pieces on all sides to seal. Add the chopped onion to the chicken, cook for 1 minute and then deglaze the pan by pouring in the red wine, stirring all the time and scraping up any sediment from the bottom of the pan. Allow the liquid to reduce over a high heat and then stir in the tomato juice, bacon, chicken stock, tarragon and the baby onions. Stir well, season with salt and pepper and continue to cook over a moderate heat, stirring from time to time, for approximately 30 minutes.

When the sauce coats the back of a spoon, remove the chicken and the baby onions and push the sauce through a very fine sieve. Return all the ingredients to the pan over a moderate heat to heat through thoroughly and then season and serve immediately.

ROSEMARY CHICKEN SURPRISE

Chicken legs are boned and stuffed for this recipe, before being braised in a well-flavoured stock.

Serves 4

4 chicken livers
4 chicken legs, boned
Salt and freshly ground black pepper
3 tbsps freshly chopped rosemary
430ml/¾ pint rich chicken stock
60g/2oz butter

Cut any veins from the chicken livers and rinse them in plenty of cold water. Spread the chicken meat out on a work surface, skin side down. Sprinkle the inside of the meat with salt, pepper and 2 tbsps of the rosemary. Place a chicken liver over the seasoning on each piece of chicken, roll the meat tightly around the liver and secure well with kitchen string. Do this for all four pieces of meat.

Heat the chicken stock with the remaining rosemary and add the chicken rolls. Cover and simmer gently for 20 minutes. Remove the chicken and keep warm. Place pan back on a high heat and allow the sauce to reduce and thicken. Reduce the heat to very low and whisk in the butter, piece, by piece. Season the sauce to taste. Cut the rolls into slices and serve on a bed of spaghetti with the sauce poured over.

COLD CHICKEN SICILIAN STYLE

Chilled caper-stuffed chicken served with potatoes and a basil-flavoured mayonnaise.

Serves 4

INGREDIENTS
4 chicken legs, boned
Salt and freshly ground black
   pepper
2 tbsps capers
1 egg yolk
½ tsp mustard
200ml/7 fl oz olive oil
5 basil leaves, cut into very thin
   strips
1 tbsp freshly chopped parsley
2 large, good quality potatoes,
   steam cooked and peeled

Season the inside of the meat with plenty of salt and pepper. Sprinkle 1 tbsp of capers over the seasoned meat, roll tightly and neatly, then secure with kitchen string. Steam-cook these rolls for approximately 10 to 15 minutes, depending on their thickness. Allow the rolls to cool and then cut them into round slices.

Prepare the mayonnaise by whisking together the egg yolk and the mustard. Add the olive oil drop by drop, whisking continuously until the oil has been used up. Season the mayonnaise with salt and pepper and add the remaining capers, the basil and parsley. Cut the potatoes into slices. Serve the potatoes and chicken with the mayonnaise dotted over.

CHICKEN CACCIATORE

Cacciatore means in the style of the hunter, and that means this dish includes mushrooms. I sometimes add a few dried mushrooms for extra flavour.

Serves 4-6

INGREDIENTS
3 tbsps olive oil
120g/4oz mushrooms, quartered if large
1.4kg/3lbs chicken, skinned if desired and cut into pieces
1 onion
2 cloves garlic
150ml/¼ pint vermouth
1 tbsp white wine vinegar
150ml/¼ pint chicken stock
1 tsp freshly chopped oregano
1 sprig fresh rosemary
400g/14oz can tomatoes
60g/2oz black olives, pitted
2 tbsps freshly chopped parsley
Salt and freshly ground black pepper

Preheat the oven to 180°C/350°F/Gas Mark 4. Heat the oil in a heavy-based frying pan and cook the mushrooms for about 1-2 minutes. Remove them and set aside. Brown the chicken in the oil and transfer the browned pieces to an ovenproof casserole.

Chop the onion and garlic finely. Pour off all but 1 tbsp of the oil in the frying pan and reheat the pan. Cook the onion and garlic until softened but not coloured. Add the vermouth and vinegar and boil to reduce by half. Add the chicken stock, tomatoes, oregano, rosemary, salt and pepper. Break up the tomatoes and bring the sauce to the boil. Allow to cook for 2 minutes.

Pour the sauce over the chicken in the casserole, cover and cook for about 1 hour.

To remove the stones from the olives, roll them on a flat surface to loosen the stones and then use a swivel vegetable peeler to extract them. Alternatively use a cherry stoner. Add the mushrooms and olives for the last 5 minutes of cooking. Remove the rosemary before serving, season to taste and sprinkle with chopped parsley.

POLLO IN DOLCE-FORTE – CHICKEN IN SWEET-SOUR SAUCE

I think 'dolce-forte' is a wonderful way of saying sweet and sour! This is a sophisticated dish of unusual flavourings.

Serves 4-6

INGREDIENTS

1 chicken weighing about
   1.8kg/4lbs
1 large onion
1 large carrot
15 juniper berries
5 tbsps maraschino liqueur
5 tbsps white wine vinegar
10 tbsps water
1 bay leaf
4 tbsps olive oil
Salt and freshly ground black
   pepper

Joint the chicken. Marinate the pieces for several hours in the chopped onion, carrot, liqueur, vinegar, water, juniper berries and bay leaf. Preheat the oven to 160°C/325°F/Gas Mark 3. Take the joints from the marinade and drain well. Sauté the chicken in the olive oil until golden, then place in a shallow casserole, and add the unstrained marinade. Cover and cook in the oven for about 1 hour or until the chicken is tender. Place on a warmed serving dish and keep warm. Remove the bay leaf and press the cooking juices through a sieve. Reheat gently, season and pour over the chicken to serve.

169

CAPON WITH GARDEN VEGETABLES

Capons are castrated cock birds and it is actually illegal to produce them in some countries, including the U.K. A large chicken cooks just as well as a capon in this recipe.

Serves 4-6

INGREDIENTS

1 capon or chicken weighing about 2.3kg/5lbs
2 slices pork fat
225g/8oz chicken livers, chopped
225g/8oz prosciutto crudo, chopped
Salt and freshly ground black pepper
120g/4oz sliced bacon, chopped
2 carrots, sliced
1 onion, sliced
Bouquet garni of parsley, thyme and rosemary
200ml/7 fl oz white wine
200ml/7 fl oz chicken stock
60g/2oz butter
1 large aubergine, diced
2 courgettes, slices
2 green peppers, cut into strips
4 stalks celery, sliced
225g/8oz mushrooms, sliced
430ml/¾ pint chopped tomato pulp or passata

Preheat the oven to 190°C/375°F/Gas Mark 5. Cover the legs of the capon with pork fat. Stuff the bird with the livers and prosciutto, then sprinkle with salt and pepper and truss. Grease a shallow casserole dish, put a layer of bacon, carrots, onion and bouquet garni in the bottom and place the capon on top. Add the wine and stock and roast in the preheated oven for 2 hours, or until tender.

Heat the butter and sauté the aubergine, courgettes, pepper and celery. After 15 minutes add the mushrooms and tomato pulp. Season with salt and pepper and continue cooking for 5 minutes.

Remove the capon from the casserole to a warmed serving plate. Press the pan juices through a strainer and boil to reduce and thicken if necessary. Serve the capon surrounded with vegetables. Season the sauce and spoon it over.

POLLO CON PEPERONI – CHICKEN WITH PEPPERS

A simple casserole of chicken and peppers with all my favourite Mediterranean flavours

Serves 4

INGREDIENTS

1 chicken, weighing about 1.15kg/2½lbs
4 to 5 fleshy green and red peppers
1 large onion, sliced
2 tbsps butter
3 tbsps olive oil
Salt and freshly ground black pepper
150ml/¼ pint dry white wine
850ml/1½ pints freshly chopped tomato pulp, or passata
225ml/8 fl oz chicken stock
A large handful freshly chopped basil

Cut the chicken into serving pieces. Roast the peppers over a gas flame or under the grill until skin blisters. Rub skins off with a kitchen towel. Remove the seeds and cut the peppers into 2.5cm/1 inch wide strips. Sauté the onion in butter and oil until softened. Add the chicken pieces and brown on both sides. Season with salt and pepper and, when the chicken has browned, add the wine. Simmer until the wine has evaporated, add the peppers, tomatoes and another pinch of salt and pepper, then the stock. Cover and simmer over a low heat, stirring occasionally, for about 45 minutes or until the chicken is tender. Remove from heat and garnish the chicken with chopped basil (or parsley if you prefer). Reduce the pan juices by rapid boiling to a thick sauce, season and pour over the chicken.

POLLO AL LATTE – CHICKEN COOKED IN MILK

Cooking in milk is an old country technique. The acid in the milk was originally useful for tenderising old chickens and tougher cuts of meat. Add more bay leaves for a memorable flavour.

Serves 4-6

INGREDIENTS
1 chicken weighing about
 1.8kg/4lbs
2 tbsps olive oil
1 onion, chopped
1 carrot, chopped
850ml/1½ pints milk
5 sprigs parsley
5 sprigs marjoram
1 sprig basil
1 bay leaf
Salt and freshly ground black
 pepper
Slivered almonds to garnish

In a large saucepan, brown the chicken in the hot oil. Remove and set aside. Sauté the onion and carrot in the oil for a few minutes until beginning to brown. Return the chicken to the pan and add the milk. Add the herbs and seasoning. Bring to the boil, cover and simmer very slowly for about 1 hour, until the chicken is tender. Place the chicken on a warmed serving plate and keep warm. Discard the bay leaf, and blend as much of the cooking juices as needed with the carrot and onion and herbs for a sauce to serve with the chicken (it should be fairly thick). Season to taste. Cut the chicken into joints, coat with the sauce, garnish with browned slivered almonds if wished.

CHICKEN TONGUE ROLLS

Don't worry – I'm not asking you to stuff chickens' tongues!
These delicious meat rolls are created from chicken, tongue
and two types of Italian cheese.

Serves 4

INGREDIENTS
4 chicken legs
4 slices of smoked tongue
2 tbsps grated Parmesan cheese
1 tbsp grated Fontina cheese
1 tbsp freshly chopped parsley
Salt and freshly ground black
  pepper
1 tbsp oil

Garnish
Parsley
Tomato

Remove the bones carefully from the chicken legs, keeping the meat in one piece. Flatten out, and divide the tongue equally between the chicken. Mix together the grated cheeses, parsley and salt and pepper to taste. Place 1 tbsp of the mixture on each piece of chicken. Roll up the chicken and tie each with string, 2 or 3 times.

Heat the oil in a pan and fry the chicken rolls gently for about 20 minutes, turning occasionally to cook evenly. Remove from the heat and allow to cool completely. Cut away the string. Slice into rounds and serve garnished with parsley and tomato.

MILANESE-STYLE OSSO BUCO

*A wonderfully rich dish of veal in a wine and tomato sauce.
I sometimes use chicken breasts when the veal is
unobtainable. Serve with Risotto Milanese.*

Serves 4

INGREDIENTS
4 slices veal knuckle
Salt and freshly ground black
   pepper
Flour for dredging
2 tbsps olive oil
1 onion, sliced
2 cloves garlic
200ml/7 fl oz white wine
430ml/¾ pint stock or water
4 tomatoes, peeled, seeded and
   roughly chopped
1 bouquet garni

Season the meat with salt and pepper and toss in the flour. Heat the oil in a large pan and brown and seal the meat. Remove the meat and in the same oil fry the onion and garlic for a few minutes. Return the meat to the pan, add the wine and allow it to reduce until it has almost all evaporated, scraping up any meat sediment from the bottom of the pan. Stir in the stock or water, tomatoes and the bouquet garni, then season with salt and pepper. Simmer gently for approximately 1½ hours until the veal is tender, checking the level of the liquid and adding water or stock as necessary. Remove the bouquet garni and serve hot.

OSSO BUCO WITH ALMOND MARSALA

Everybody has tasted osso buco, but the addition of Marsala flavoured with almonds really brings this dish to life.

Serves 4

INGREDIENTS
4 thick slices of veal knuckle (with the bone)
1 onion, sliced
1 clove garlic, chopped
120ml/4 fl oz almond flavoured Marsala
430ml/¾ pint chicken stock
75ml/3 fl oz crushed tomato pulp
1 bay leaf
30ml/2 tbsps olive oil
Salt and freshly ground black pepper

Heat the oil and gently fry the onions, garlic and the slices of veal until slightly coloured. Remove the excess fat with absorbent kitchen paper and deglaze the pan with the Marsala. Allow to reduce a little and then stir in the stock, tomato pulp and the bay leaf. Pour over enough water to cover the meat. Season with salt and pepper and cook until the meat is tender and cooked through – about 1½-2 hours. Serve hot with the sauce poured over.

VEAL IN ORANGE

The orange in this recipe gives a really Mediterranean flavour and makes a welcome change from lemon seasoning. Use chopped chicken breasts as an alternative to veal.

Serves 4

INGREDIENTS
1kg/2¼lbs veal fillet
1 onion
570ml/1 pint chicken stock
Salt and freshly ground black
  pepper
2 oranges
4 small, young carrots
225g/8oz arborio rice
60g/2oz butter
45g/1½oz flour
Pinch of powdered saffron
150ml/¼ pint double cream
Parsley to garnish

Dice the veal. Peel the onion and keep it whole. Place the veal, onion, stock and seasoning in a pan, and bring to the boil. Lower the heat and simmer for 40 minutes, until the meat is tender. Remove and discard the onion.

Cut away the peel from 1 orange, remove the white pith, then cut the orange peel into narrow strips. Soak in 150ml/¼ pint water for 30 minutes. Peel the carrots, cut into neat matchsticks, put with the orange rind and water and a little seasoning and simmer in a covered pan for 20 minutes. Remove the carrots and orange rind and cook the rice in the remaining juices and salted water.

Heat the butter in a pan, stir in the flour and cook for several minutes. Add the strained veal stock and bring to the boil, stirring continuously. Cook until thickened, then add the orange rind, carrots, cooked rice and remaining liquid, together with the pinch of saffron powder and the cream. Stir over a low heat until smooth. Add the cooked veal and mix thoroughly. Arrange a border of rice with the remaining orange cut into slices on a serving dish. Spoon the veal mixture in the centre of the dish and sprinkle with parsley.

VEAL MARENGO

The classic 'Marengo' dish is made with chicken, and is really French as it was created by Napoleon's chef. However, Marengo is in Italy, north of Genoa, so here is an Italian version of the dish using veal.

Serves 4

INGREDIENTS
460g/1lb neck of veal
Seasoned flour
90g/3oz butter
2 onions, chopped
280ml/½ pint white stock
225g/8oz tomatoes, skinned and
    chopped
60g/2oz mushrooms, chopped
Salt and freshly ground black
    pepper

Garnish
4 slices of bread, cut into
    croûtons
Oil for frying
Parsley
Lemon

Cut the veal into cubes. Coat with seasoned flour and fry until golden brown in the hot butter. Add the onion and fry until transparent, then add the stock, tomatoes and mushrooms. Season well. Simmer gently for about 1 hour. Serve garnished with croûtons of fried bread, parsley and lemon wedges.

ESCALOPES WITH CHEESE

These escalopes are filled with Parma ham and cheese before frying, and are truly delicious!

Serves 4

INGREDIENTS
4 veal escalopes
4 slices Parma ham
8 slices Fontina, Cheddar or
  other soft cheese
Salt and freshly ground black
  pepper
 Flour for dredging
1 egg, beaten
120g/4oz fresh breadcrumbs
3 tbsps oil
30g/1oz butter

Preheat the oven to 180°C/350°F/Gas Mark 4. Flatten the escalopes between 2 sheets of greaseproof paper, gently tapping them with the flat side of a long knife. Remove the paper. Place a slice of ham over each escalope and then 2 pieces of cheese. Roll the escalopes up firmly, so that the cheese and ham are well covered. Season with salt and pepper, and roll the escalopes in the flour, then dip them in the beaten egg. Shake off any excess egg and roll in the breadcrumbs, making sure that the escalopes are well covered.

Heat the oil and butter together in a frying pan and fry the escalopes until crisp and golden brown. Transfer to an ovenproof dish and finish cooking in a medium oven for 10-15 minutes. Serve hot.

SHOULDER OF VEAL
WITH TRUFFLES

This is a luxurious dish but quite simple and straight-forward to prepare.

Serves 4

INGREDIENTS
1 thick rasher smoked bacon
2 medium truffles
1 tbsp oil
30g/1oz butter
1 onion, sliced
570g/1¼lbs shoulder of veal, cut into cubes
60ml/2 fl oz white wine
Salt and freshly ground black pepper

Cut the bacon into small pieces. Grate the truffles finely onto a plate. Heat the oil and butter together in a large pan and gently fry the onion and bacon for a few minutes. Add the veal and cook until browned all over. Tip out any excess fat, add the wine and allow it to evaporate almost completely. Season with salt and pepper, add water to cover and simmer for approximately 45 minutes, or until the sauce reduces to just below the level of the meat. Stir in the grated truffle, mix well, season and serve.

VEAL IN MARJORAM SAUCE

*Marjoram is an excellent seasoning for veal and this recipe,
where the sauce is made without cream, is not too rich.*

Serves 4

INGREDIENTS

4 veal escalopes, cut into very
thin slices
Salt and freshly ground black
pepper
Flour for dredging
2 tbsps olive oil
½ onion, finely chopped
2 large mushrooms, cut into very
thin slices
1 clove garlic, chopped
1 tbsp freshly chopped marjoram
2 tsps freshly chopped parsley
175ml/6 fl oz chicken stock

Season the thin slices of veal
with salt and pepper, then toss
them in the flour, shaking off any
excess. Heat the oil in a frying
pan and gently fry the onion,
mushrooms and garlic for a few
minutes. Add the veal, marjoram
and parsley. Stir and turn the
slices of meat over once. Pour in
the stock and cook until it
reduces to a thickish sauce.
Shake and stir the contents of the
pan occasionally. Taste if
necessary, then adjust the
seasoning, and serve hot.

VEAL WITH MARSALA SAUCE

Marsala is the secret ingredient in many Italian dishes – use a sweet sherry if Marsala is not available.

Serves 4

INGREDIENTS
2 tbsps olive oil
1 large onion, finely sliced
900g/2lbs shoulder of veal, cut into cubes
60ml/2 fl oz almond-flavoured Marsala
1 sprig rosemary
Salt and freshly ground black pepper

Heat the oil in a large pan and fry the onion and veal until the meat is sealed all over and well browned. Add the Marsala and cook until almost evaporated, stirring up any sediment from the bottom of the pan. Add sufficient water to cover the meat completely. Add the rosemary to the pan, season with salt and pepper and simmer gently for 45 minutes, or until the meat is tender. Remove from the heat and serve the meat with the sauce poured over. Reduce the sauce by fast boiling, if necessary, and season before serving.

VEAL IN CREAM SAUCE

This makes a rich but delicate dish – the cream sauce is not at all strong and does not dwarf the flavour of the veal.

Serves 4

INGREDIENTS

3 tbsps olive oil
1 onion, finely sliced
680g/1½lbs shoulder of veal
200ml/7 fl oz chicken stock
½ tsp dried marjoram
1 egg yolk
150ml/¼ pint single cream
1 tsp lemon juice
Salt and freshly ground black
  pepper

Heat the oil in a frying pan and gently fry the onion for 1 minute. Add the meat to the frying pan and sauté until lightly browned. Tip out any excess fat and pour the contents of the pan into a flameproof casserole. Add the stock to the casserole and add sufficient water to cover the meat. Add the marjoram and stir. Cover and simmer slowly for approximately 1 hour and 15 minutes, checking the meat for tenderness and adding water should the level of liquid drop too much.

Beat the egg yolk into the cream. Remove the meat from the casserole and keep it warm. Whisk the cream mixture into the sauce, and continue whisking over a gentle heat until the sauce thickens. Remove immediately from the heat, stir in the lemon juice, season with salt and pepper, pour over the meat and serve.

VEAL SCALOPPINE WITH PROSCIUTTO AND CHEESE

Veal is the most popular meat in Italy, but chicken or turkey may be used if preferred. Very tender lean pork is another alternative.

Serves 4

INGREDIENTS

8 veal escalopes
30g/1oz butter or margarine
1 clove garlic, crushed
8 slices prosciutto ham
3 tbsps sherry
150ml/¼ pint beef stock
1 sprig rosemary
8 slices Mozzarella cheese
Salt and freshly ground black
  pepper

Pound the veal escalopes until thin, between two pieces of greaseproof paper, with a meat mallet or a rolling pin. Melt the butter or margarine in a sauté pan and add the veal and garlic. Cook until the veal is lightly browned on both sides.

Place a piece of prosciutto on top of each piece of veal and add the sherry, stock and sprig of rosemary to the pan. Cover the pan and cook the veal for about 10 minutes over a gentle heat, or until cooked. Remove the meat to a heatproof serving dish and top each piece of veal with a slice of cheese. Bring the cooking liquid from the veal to the boil and allow it to boil rapidly until slightly reduced. Meanwhile, place the veal under a preheated grill to melt and brown the cheese. Remove the sprig of rosemary from the sauce and pour the sauce around the meat to serve.

VITELLO TONNATO – VEAL WITH TUNA

One of my favourite summer dishes – perfect for easy entertaining. Turkey is also popular when cooked in this way. I usually try to leave the veal in the tuna sauce overnight, so that the flavours have a chance to blend.

Serves 4-6

INGREDIENTS

570g/1¼lbs boneless breast or
   shoulder of veal, in one piece
Salt
1 stick celery, chopped
1 carrot
2 tbsps chopped parsley
1 tbsp onion, chopped
200g/7oz can tuna, drained and
   flaked
280ml/½ pint mayonnaise
2 tbsps capers
2 anchovy fillets in oil
150ml/¼ pint dry white wine
1 lemon, cut into slices
1 carrot, sliced and cooked
2 pickled gherkins

Trim any membranes from the veal. Put a little water and a few pinches of salt in a saucepan; add the celery, carrot, parsley and onion. Bring to the boil, then add the veal. Simmer for 1 to 1½ hours, or until the veal is tender. Drain and set aside to cool.

Blend the tuna with the mayonnaise, half the capers and the anchovy fillets in a liquidiser or food processor. Beat in the wine, which serves not only to smooth the sauce but to whiten it. Slice the cold veal and lay slices, overlapping, on a serving platter. Cover with tuna sauce. Sprinkle with the remaining capers and garnish with half slices of lemon, boiled carrot slices and thin slices of gherkin. This sauce is also excellent on boiled beef.

OSELETI SCAMPAI –
SKEWERED VEAL BIRDS

*These are very meaty and substantial kebabs. Serve with
plenty of salad and warm Italian bread, as an alternative to
polenta. The kebabs may also be grilled or barbecued.*

Serves 4

INGREDIENTS

225g/8oz lean veal steak, cubed
225g/8oz fresh ham steak, cubed
120g/4oz pork liver, cubed
120g/4oz bacon, cubed
Fresh sage leaves
3 tbsps oil
7 tbsps dry white wine
150ml/¼ pint stock

Place the veal, ham, liver and
bacon cubes on long skewers,
alternating various kinds of meat
and occasionally putting a sage
leaf between one piece and
another. Heat oil in a frying pan,
add the skewers and cook over
high heat, turning occasionally.
Add the white wine and stock
and cook for another 10 minutes,
turning occasionally. Serve on a
bed of polenta.

MEAT & GAME

The Italians have always been big meat eaters and there are records of their feasts going back to ancient times, describing banquets of beef, veal, pork, sausages and various game birds and animals. Meat is still enjoyed today in great variety, and even the smallest butcher will keep a good stock of game as well as the more usual meats.

Ancient Markets and Modern Stores

Owing to the generally conservative nature of the British shopper it has taken the supermarket chains many years to introduce a reasonable range of game to their shelves. The modern Italian supermarkets have had to include a good range for many years as all such meats are extremely popular – it is necessary to include at least rabbit and game birds if a store is to succeed in luring the shopper away from the more traditional market. In the markets such birds will be displayed in feather but dead, whereas in France many are still live in the markets. It is, however, in the markets where the discerning shopper will find such delicacies as wild boar, often displayed with large sprigs of bay leaves in their mouths as bay is the traditional garnish for the roasted meat.

Beef, geese, turkey, pork and many pork products are all widely available, as are game birds. An alarming selection of smaller birds, such as larks, are also easily obtainable. Small birds are generally roasted on a skewer and consumed as a great delicacy, a practice which I shall never come to terms with. Deer, hare and boar are common in the country regions of Italy and feature widely in classic regional recipes.

The tradition of the meat market – which is under threat from the modern supermarket, even in Italy – is an ancient Italian institution from the time of the Roman Empire. The remains of the first major food market can still be seen in the Forum of Trajan in Rome, where the butchers of the time set up their stalls in and around the main market in the Forum.

The Influence of Ancient Rome

As the Roman armies moved through Europe, pushing out the boundaries of the Empire, many Roman customs were introduced to the newly colonised lands, and many foods and recipes from the new territories were taken back to Rome, for the cooks of the day to experiment with. Thus Italian cookery was made into the varied and exciting cuisine that we know today.

Many of the recipes used to celebrate the triumphs of Ancient Rome have been adapted to become the standard classic dishes of today. The Romans had something of a reputation for gluttony but then banquets were the most extraordinary occasions throughout the ancient world.

There is still plenty of good food in Italy and the classic dishes show an instinctive and inventive ability to mix ingredients and flavourings in many memorable dishes.

Olives and Anchovies for Flavouring

I have to confess to not being a great fan of rabbit but the

Italians make a delicious dish of Rabbit Stuffed with Olives. The olives impart a wonderful flavour which blends beautifully with the rabbit – I would recommend a mix of green and black olives for such a dish, with rather more green than black. This may be further developed with the addition of walnuts and a little of the traditional rabbit seasoning of mustard – try the recipe for Walnut Rabbit.

Veal and beef have both been extremely popular in Italy since culinary records began. Veal is usually cooked in a light or fragrant sauce whereas the Italians have many robust and hearty recipes for cooking beef. As in the French cuisine many of these recipes reflect the other produce of the region of their origin – it is important to use the wine and seasonings of the area in order to produce the correct blend of flavours that has made the dish a classic.

Duck is also a regular feature on Italian menus, both in the home and in restaurants. Roasted or casseroled it is delicious but my preference, and that of most Italians, is always for wild duck which has darker meat, a more gamy flavour and much less fat. I have already mentioned that olives make a wonderful seasoning for rabbit and they are just as good with duck, especially mixed with anchovy fillets. Anchovies, prominent in all Italian cookery, provide an excellent foil for any very rich meats as their salty flavour cuts through and balances the richness.

ARISTA DI MAIALE –
SADDLE OF PORK TUSCAN
STYLE

*A simple recipe with a delicious flavour. Try the pork hot one
day and cold the next.*

Serves 4-6

INGREDIENTS
1.15kg/2½lbs pork joint
2 cloves garlic, cut into slivers
2 sprigs fresh rosemary
Salt and freshly ground black
    pepper
4 tbsps olive oil

Preheat the oven to
220°C/425°F/Gas Mark 7. Make
small slits in the pork and stuff
with slivers of garlic and tufts of
rosemary. Season with salt and
freshly ground pepper. Heat 2
tbsps of the oil in a roasting tin.
Add the pork, pour a thin stream
of remaining oil over it and roast
in the preheated oven for about
20 minutes. When the pork is
nicely browned, lower the heat
to 180°C/350°F/Gas Mark 4 and
roast for a further 1¼ hours,
turning the meat occasionally.
Remove from the oven, carve
and arrange the slices on a
serving platter to serve. This dish
is good either hot or cold.

HERBY PORK CHOPS

A complete dish of garlic and parsley seasoned pork, served with sautéed potatoes.

Serves 4

INGREDIENTS

4 pork chops
Salt and freshly ground black
  pepper
2 cloves garlic, chopped
4 tbsps freshly chopped parsley
4 large good quality potatoes
4 tbsps oil
2 knobs butter

Preheat the oven to 180°C/350°F/Gas Mark 4. Bone the chops and season the meat with plenty of salt and pepper. Sprinkle the garlic and parsley over the chops, pressing the seasonings well into the meat. Place the meat in the refrigerator until required.

Peel the potatoes and cut them into thin slices. Heat 2 tbsps oil and 1 knob of butter in a large frying pan. Sauté the potatoes, adding any leftover garlic and parsley to the pan, until cooked through. Meanwhile, fry the pork chops in the remaining oil and butter, browning them on all sides, and then finish cooking the pork in a medium oven until cooked through, about 10 minutes. Serve the chops hot with the sautéed potatoes.

ROAST PORK FILLET WITH ROSEMARY

Rosemary is often cooked with lamb but it is also an excellent seasoning for pork. This is a good dish for entertaining as it can be prepared in advance and requires very little attention during cooking.

Serves 4

INGREDIENTS
Rectangular strip of pork fat
2 cloves garlic, chopped
1 sprig rosemary, chopped
½ tsp coarse sea salt
Freshly ground black pepper
Few leaves tarragon
800g/1¾lbs pork fillet
1 tbsp oil

Preheat the oven to 200°C/400°F/Gas Mark 6. Spread out the fat and sprinkle with the garlic, rosemary, sea salt, pepper and tarragon. Place the pork fillet in the centre of the prepared fat, then roll the fat around the meat. Secure with kitchen string.

Brush an ovenproof dish with oil, add the pork fillet and roast in the hot oven for 45 minutes. Turn the pork over once, halfway through cooking. Serve either hot or cold, cut into thick slices with the cooking juices spooned over.

PORK ROULADES WITH POLENTA

Polenta has long been the staple starchy food of Italy, especially in country dishes. This recipe makes the polenta in the traditional way but quick-cook varieties are available in most supermarkets.

Serves 4-8

INGREDIENTS

225g/8oz coarse yellow cornmeal
1.7 litres/3 pints chicken stock
Salt and white pepper

Roulades
8 pork escalopes or steaks
8 slices Parma ham
4 large cup mushrooms
4 tbsps grated Parmesan cheese
1 tbsp freshly chopped sage
Seasoned flour for dredging
4 tbsps olive oil

1 small onion, finely chopped
2 sticks celery, finely chopped
1 clove garlic, crushed
90ml/3 fl oz brown stock
150ml/¼ pint dry white wine
120g/4oz canned plum tomatoes, drained and juice reserved
1 tsp tomato purée
Salt and freshly ground black pepper
90ml/3 fl oz dry Marsala
Fresh sage leaves for garnish

Bring the chicken stock for the polenta to the boil in a large stock pot and start adding the cornmeal in a very slow, steady stream, stirring continuously. Add salt and pepper and continue cooking over very low heat, stirring frequently, for about 55 minutes.

Flatten the pork escalopes or steaks and place a slice of Parma ham on top of each. Chop the mushrooms and divide among the pork escalopes, spooning on top of the ham slices. Sprinkle with the Parmesan cheese and the fresh sage. Fold the sides of the pork escalopes into the centre to seal them, and roll up the pork like a Swiss roll. Secure each roll with a cocktail stick. Dredge each roulade in flour, shaking off the excess.

Heat the olive oil in a large sautée pan or frying pan and add the pork roulades, seam side down. Cook on all sides until browned. Remove the roulades and keep them warm.

Add the onion and celery to the oil in the pan and cook until lightly browned. Add the garlic and all the remaining ingredients except the Marsala. Reserve the juice from the tomatoes for later use if necessary. Bring the sauce to the boil, breaking up the tomatoes. Return the roulades to the pan, cover and cook over a moderate heat for about 15-20 minutes or until the pork is completely cooked. Add the reserved tomato juice, as necessary, if the liquid evaporates.

When the pork is cooked, remove it to a dish and keep it warm. Add the Marsala to the sauce and bring to the boil. Allow to boil for 5-10 minutes. The sauce may be puréed in a food processor and also sieved if desired.

To assemble the dish, spoon the polenta onto a serving plate. Remove the cocktail sticks from the roulades and place on top of the polenta. Spoon the sauce over the meat and garnish the dish with fresh sage leaves.

POLPETTE ROMAINE – ROMAN MEATBALLS

The Italians make wonderful meatballs. I suggest serving these on a bed of buttered tagliatelle.

Serves 4

INGREDIENTS
340g/12oz plain flour
2 eggs, beaten
90g/3oz grated Parmesan cheese
225ml/8 fl oz milk
120g/4oz butter
Salt
120g/4oz ham, minced
460g/1lb Mozzarella, grated

Preheat the oven to 190°C/375°F/Gas Mark 5. In a saucepan mix together the flour, eggs and Parmesan. Gradually stir in the milk. Place the saucepan over a low heat and beat in half the butter and a pinch of salt. Cool. Turn the dough onto a floured board and knead a few times until it becomes a smooth ball.

Take 2 tbsps of the ham and Mozzarella and, using the palms of your hands, roll it into a ball about as large as a walnut. Pinch off pieces of dough and flatten to 6mm/¼ inch thickness. Wrap the ham and cheese ball in dough to cover it completely. Continue until you have used up all the ham and all the dough. Butter a shallow ovenproof dish and add the meatballs in a single layer. Dot each with a little of the remaining butter. Bake in the preheated oven for about 30 minutes or until brown.

SCALOPPINE ALLA TOSCANA – BEEF ESCALOPES TUSCAN STYLE

Thin slices of tender beef in a rich wine and tomato sauce, garnished with anchovies and capers. Roll the capers in the anchovies if you have the time.

Serves 4

INGREDIENTS
680g/1½lbs boneless beef e.g. topside, sliced 6mm/¼ inch thick
Salt
Plain flour
1 egg, beaten
45g/1½oz butter
2 tbsps olive oil
90ml/3 fl oz Marsala
1 tbsp tomato paste
4 anchovy fillets, chopped
1 tbsp capers, chopped

Pound the beef until very thin, then sprinkle with salt and flour on both sides. Dip the beef in beaten egg. Heat the butter and oil in a large frying pan, then add the beef and brown on both sides. Add the Marsala, raise the heat slightly, and simmer until the wine evaporates. Place the beef slices on a platter and keep them warm. Add the tomato paste mixed with 120ml/4 fl oz of water to the pan and simmer for 5 minutes. Add the anchovies and capers and simmer for 2 minutes more. Return the beef to the pan and simmer for 2-3 minutes over a low heat. Garnish with rolled up anchovies with capers in the centre.

BISTECCHE AL PICCANTINO – FILET MIGNON PIQUANT

A delicious way of serving steaks – I am always rather disappointed in steaks served without a tasty sauce.

Serves 4

INGREDIENTS
120g/4oz black olives
3 anchovy fillets, chopped
225ml/8 fl oz chopped tomato
    pulp or passata
4 fillet mignon steaks weighing
    about 175g/6oz each
3 tbsps olive oil
2 tbsps capers
150ml/¼ pint dry white wine
Salt and freshly ground black
    pepper

Pit the olives and chop them coarsely. Mix the olives, anchovy fillets and tomato pulp. Brown steaks quickly on both sides in the oil and remove to a plate. Add the tomato pulp mixture and the capers to the pan juices. Heat until simmering. Stir in the wine and a pinch of pepper and simmer until the sauce is thick. Season to taste with salt. Return the steaks to the pan and cook to your preference, turning several times in the sauce and making sure that they are not overcooked. Salt lightly and serve immediately with the pan juices spooned over them.

BEEF IN BAROLO

*Barolo is one of my favourite Italian wines. It is produced in
Piedmont, in north west Italy, and seems to be at its best
between 5 and 10 years old.*

Serves 4

INGREDIENTS
1 carrot, sliced
1 onion, sliced
½ leek, sliced
1 sprig thyme
1 sprig rosemary
1 bay leaf
2 cloves garlic
5 peppercorns
2 tsps tomato purée
1 bottle Barolo wine
900g/2lbs silverside beef
3 tbsps olive oil
570ml/1 pint water or beef stock
Salt and freshly ground black
    pepper

Mix together the carrot, onion,
leek, thyme, rosemary, bay leaf,
garlic, peppercorns, a little
ground pepper, tomato purée
and the wine. Add the meat and
marinate overnight.

Drain the meat, heat the olive oil
in a large pan and seal the meat
on all sides until lightly browned.
Tip out any excess fat and add
the marinade, boiling until it is
slightly reduced. Add the water
or stock, and season with salt
and pepper. Simmer gently for 2
hours. Test the meat for
tenderness and continue cooking
if necessary, adding more water
if required.

Cut the beef into slices, strain the
sauce and serve the beef with the
sauce poured over.

PIEDMONT BEEF CASSEROLE

A rich casserole from northern Italy, flavoured with smoked sausage, juniper and vegetables.

Serves 4

INGREDIENTS
250ml/9 fl oz chicken stock
460g/1lb lean shoulder of beef
1 large smoked sausage (or a few
  small ones)
225g/8oz veal knuckle
3 carrots
½ leek, thinly sliced
1 onion, stuck with 1 clove
4 juniper berries
1 bouquet garni
Salt and freshly ground black
  pepper
2 courgettes

Heat the stock in a large flameproof casserole, add an equal quantity of water and the beef, sausage and veal joint. Add 1 carrot, cut into thin rounds, the leek, onion, juniper berries, bay leaf and the bouquet garni. Season with salt and pepper, add water to cover completely, and simmer for 2½ hours.

Meanwhile, cut the remaining carrots and the courgettes into oval shapes and steam them for a few minutes – they should still be quite crisp. When the casserole is cooked, remove the meat and cut it into thin slices. Place the meat on a warmed serving dish. Cut the sausage into rounds and the meat and fat off the joint into small cubes, and add to the beef. Strain the juices into a clean saucepan through a very fine sieve, and season to taste. Add the steamed vegetables to the pan and heat through. Serve the vegetables around the cut meats, with the sauce poured over.

198

TUSCANY BEEF

Tuscany is a colourful region producing some wonderful food. This recipe makes full use of the local produce.

Serves 4

INGREDIENTS

900g/2lbs braising steak, cut into small cubes
Flour for dredging
3 tbsps olive oil
1 clove garlic, chopped
½ tsp freshly chopped rosemary
430ml/¾ pint red wine
2 tbsps tomato purée
Salt and freshly ground black pepper

Toss the meat in the flour. Heat the oil in a flameproof casserole, add the garlic, meat and rosemary and fry on all sides until the meat is well browned. Add the red wine and boil, stirring, until slightly reduced, then pour in enough water to cover the meat. Stir in the tomato purée, season with salt and pepper, cover and simmer gently for approximately 2 hours. Check the meat for tenderness and remove from the heat when cooked through. Season to taste. Serve hot.

AGNELLO AL FORNO – SICILIAN ROAST LAMB

There was an Italian restaurant called 'Al Forno's' that we used from college – it simply means in the fire, or cooked in the oven.

Serves 4-6

INGREDIENTS

1 leg of lamb, about 1.6kg/3½lbs in weight
60g/2oz boiled ham, diced
1-2 sprigs rosemary
250g/9oz butter, melted
3 tbsps soft breadcrumbs
225g/8oz grated cheese
Salt and freshly ground black pepper

Preheat the oven to 190°C/375°F/Gas Mark 5. With a sharp knife, make incisions into the surface of the lamb, about 2.5cm/1 inch deep. Into each cut press a piece of ham and two or three leaves of rosemary. Put the meat in a roasting tin, season with salt and pepper and pour over the melted butter. Mix the breadcrumbs and the grated cheese and spread evenly over the meat, pressing down well. Roast in the preheated oven for about 1½ hours, basting from time to time. Stand for 10 minutes before carving.

LAMB CHOPS CALABRIAN

The dish relies on traditional Italian seasonings: anchovies and capers with preserved mushrooms and artichokes. The mushrooms and artichokes may be added to the pan and heated through briefly before serving.

Serves 4

INGREDIENTS
8 loin lamb chops
Salt and freshly ground black pepper
Plain flour
5 tbsps oil
8 anchovy fillets
2 tbsps capers
120g/4oz canned mushrooms, drained
4 canned artichoke hearts in oil, drained

Pound the chops to flatten them slightly. Sprinkle with salt and pepper, then dip into the flour. Heat the oil in a frying pan and brown the chops for 2-3 minutes on each side over a high heat. Drain on absorbent kitchen paper. Arrange on a serving platter and garnish with anchovy fillets, capers, mushrooms and artichoke hearts.

LAMB WITH FENNEL

A light, summery casserole flavoured with white wine and lemon juice. Thicken the sauce very slowly to prevent it from becoming grainy.

Serves 4

INGREDIENTS
680g/1½lbs boneless leg of lamb
Salt and freshly ground black
  pepper
120g/4oz fennel
2 onions, finely sliced
3 tbsps olive oil
120ml/4 fl oz white wine
1 egg yolk
1 tbsp water
½ lemon

Cut the meat into cubes and season them with salt and pepper. Cut the fennel into rounds and fry gently with the onion and lamb in the olive oil until slightly coloured. Add the white wine and allow it to reduce somewhat, stirring up any sediment from the bottom of the pan, before covering the ingredients with water. Bring to the boil, cover, reduce the heat and simmer gently for approximately 1 hour and 45 minutes. Check the level of the liquid during cooking, and add water as necessary.

Meanwhile, beat together the egg yolk, 1 tbsp water and the juice of ½ a lemon. When the casserole is cooked and the meat is quite tender, remove the lamb and, over a low heat, whisk the egg yolk mixture into the sauce, whisking continuously until the mixture thickens. Season to taste. Put the meat back into the sauce and serve hot.

MUTTON CHOPS IN RICH SAUCE

The mutton is cooked in a rich sauce with plenty of garlic. If mutton is not available use neck of lamb, or lamb loin chops.

Serves 4

INGREDIENTS
4 mutton chops (from the neck)
Salt and freshly ground black
   pepper
2 tbsps olive oil
2 slices Parma ham
½ onion, sliced
1 clove garlic, chopped
120ml/4 fl oz white wine
1 sprig thyme
1 bay leaf
1 egg yolk
Juice of ½ lemon

Season the chops with salt and pepper and toss them in the flour, shaking off any excess. Heat the oil and fry the chops on all sides to seal and brown. Cut the ham into small dice and add to the pan. Add the onion and garlic and cook for 1 minute.

Deglaze the pan with the wine and keep stirring over the heat until the wine has almost completely evaporated. Pour in sufficient water to cover, and add the thyme, bay leaf, salt and pepper. Cook for 1 hour, stirring from time to time.

Whisk together the egg yolk and the lemon juice. Remove the meat from the pan with a slotted spoon and stir the egg yolk and lemon juice into the pan juices, stirring continuously over a very gentle heat until the sauce thickens. Take off the heat, remove the sprig of thyme and the bay leaf, and replace the meat. Serve immediately.

ANATRA AL SALE – ROAST DUCK IN COARSE SALT

Roasting in salt retains all the meat juices and is a very moist and succulent way of cooking.

Serves 4

INGREDIENTS
1 duckling weighing about
    2.3kg/5lbs
Coast salt – sea salt, kosher salt
    or rock salt, about 2.3kg/5lbs

Preheat the oven to 220°C/425°F/ Gas Mark 7. Remove the giblets and reserve for making gravy. Truss to secure the legs and wings close to the body. Cover the bottom of deep roasting tin with salt to a depth of 1.25cm/ ½ inch. Sit the duckling on the salt and then cover completely with more salt, pressing down to seal the duckling. Bake in the preheated oven for 1½ hours. Scrape the salt off the surface of the duckling with a spoon, then grasp the trussing cord to lift the duckling from the salt with a quick decisive movement. Remove any final grains of salt with a pastry brush. Carve and serve.

ANATRA IN SALMI –
DUCK CASSEROLE

A salmi, a rich casserole of game birds, is a very traditional way of cooking duck. Like so many classic recipes, this sounds impressive but is very simple to prepare.

Serves 4-6

INGREDIENTS
1 duckling weighing about
   2.3kg/5lbs
1 onion
2 cloves
1 bay leaf
2 sage leaves
150ml/¼ pint olive oil
60ml/2 fl oz wine vinegar
60ml/2 fl oz dry white wine
Salt and freshly ground black
   pepper
Parsley for garnish

Joint the duckling. In a deep saucepan, place the chopped duck liver, heart and gizzard, the onion stuck with cloves, the bay leaf and sage. Place the duck on top and add the olive oil, wine vinegar and white wine. Season with salt and pepper. Cover and simmer for about 1 hour or until the duck is tender. Arrange the joints on a serving dish and keep warm. Remove the cloves and the bay leaf, and purée the remaining ingredients in the casserole with the cooking liquid in a liquidiser or food processor. Return to the heat, pour over the duck and garnish with chopped parsley.

TURKEY KEBABS

Sage is an excellent seasoning for poultry, redolent of long summer days in the Mediterranean sun. The bacon is easier to wrap around the turkey if you stretch it with the back of a knife first.

Serves 6

INGREDIENTS

1.4kg/3lbs turkey meat
2 tsps freshly chopped sage
1 sprig rosemary
Juice of 1 lemon
2 tbsps olive oil
Salt and freshly ground black
  pepper
120g/4oz streaky bacon, rinds
  and bones removed
Whole sage leaves for garnish

Remove any bones from the turkey and cut the meat into evenly-sized pieces. Combine the chopped sage, rosemary, lemon juice, oil, salt and pepper in a large bowl and add the turkey meat. Stir once or twice to coat evenly. Then cover and leave in the refrigerator overnight.

Preheat the oven to 200°C/400°F/Gas Mark 6. Cut the bacon rashers in half, stretch them with the back of a knife and wrap around some of the pieces of turkey. Leave other pieces of turkey unwrapped. Thread the bacon-wrapped turkey, plain turkey and whole sage leaves onto skewers, alternating the ingredients. Cook in the preheated oven for about 40 minutes. Alternatively, cook for 30 minutes and place the kebabs under a preheated grill for 10 minutes to crisp the bacon. Baste frequently with the marinade while cooking. Pour any remaining marinade and pan juices over the kebabs to serve.

TURKEY MARSALA

Marsala is an Italian dessert wine but, just as sherry makes an excellent seasoning for poultry, so does Marsala. It is also used extensively with veal in Italy. Don't overcook the turkey, especially if using escalopes.

Serves 4

INGREDIENTS

4 turkey breast fillets or
   escalopes
60g/2oz butter or margarine
1 clove garlic
4 anchovy fillets, soaked in milk
Capers
4 slices Mozzarella cheese
2 tsps freshly chopped marjoram
1 tbsp freshly chopped parsley
3 tbsps Marsala
150ml/¼ pint double cream
Salt and freshly ground black
   pepper

Flatten the turkey breasts between two sheets of greaseproof paper with a meat mallet or rolling pin. Escalopes will not need flattening. Melt the butter in a sauté pan and, when foaming, add the garlic and the turkey. Cook the turkey for a few minutes on each side until lightly browned, then remove it from the pan.

Drain the anchovy fillets and rinse them well. Dry on absorbent kitchen paper. Put a slice of cheese on top of each turkey fillet and arrange the anchovies and capers on top of the cheese. Sprinkle with the chopped herbs and return the turkey to the pan. Cook the turkey for a further 5 minutes over a moderate heat, until the turkey is cooked and the cheese has melted. Remove to a serving dish and keep warm. Return the pan to the heat and add the Marsala. Scrape the browned pan juices off the bottom and reduce the heat. Add the cream and whisk in well. Lower the heat and simmer gently, uncovered, for a few minutes to thicken the sauce. Season the sauce with salt and pepper and spoon over the turkey fillets to serve.

RABBIT AND LIVER SURPRISE

This recipe uses rabbit thighs which are boned and then stuffed. After being marinated, the rabbit is simmered in a well flavoured stock.

Serves 4

INGREDIENTS
4 rabbit thighs
2 rabbit livers
1 tsp chopped rosemary
1 tsp dried chopped sage
4 juniper berries
3 tbsps olive oil
200ml/7 fl oz chicken stock
Salt and freshly ground black
  pepper

Bone the rabbit thighs, keeping the meat in one piece. Cut the livers in half and place one piece on each thigh. Roll up the thighs and secure with thin kitchen string. Mix together the rosemary, sage, juniper berries and the olive oil in a large bowl and add the rabbit thighs, leaving them to marinate in the mixture for an hour.

Heat half of the marinade in a frying pan and seal the meat briskly on all sides. Pour off the oil from the frying pan, add the stock, cover and simmer gently for approximately 25 minutes. When cooked, season with salt and pepper, cut the rabbit in slices and serve on a preheated dish with the cooking juices poured over.

WALNUT RABBIT

Rabbit is often served flavoured with mustard but the addition of walnuts, wine, olives and cream make this a truly memorable dish.

Serves 4

INGREDIENTS

2 tbsps olive oil
1 onion, finely chopped
1 small stick celery, finely chopped
1 rabbit, boned and the meat cut into small pieces
15 green olives, stoned and finely chopped
15 walnuts, shelled
430ml/¾ pint white wine
430ml/¾ chicken stock
Salt and freshly ground black pepper
½ tsp mustard
2 tbsps double cream

Heat the oil in a flameproof casserole, add the onion and celery and fry until tender. Add the rabbit meat, stir and then add the olives and walnuts. Cook for 5 minutes, stirring frequently. Pour in the wine and cook over a high heat until the wine has almost evaporated, stirring up any sediment from the bottom of the pan. Pour in the stock and add a little water to cover. Season with salt and pepper, and cook over a low heat until the rabbit is tender and the juices somewhat reduced. This will take about 30 minutes. Remove the meat and whisk in the mustard and cream; do not allow the sauce to boil. Replace the meat, season, stir and serve.

OLIVE-STUFFED RABBIT MEAT

The Italians often serve rabbit with olives – it is a delicious combination of flavours.

Serves 4

INGREDIENTS
2 saddles of rabbit
½ tsp chopped rosemary
Salt and freshly ground black
   pepper
1 clove garlic, chopped
3 tbsps chopped olives
2 tbsps olive oil
3 large tomatoes, peeled, seeded
   and chopped
120ml/4 fl oz chicken stock
120ml/4 fl oz tomato juice

Remove the bones from the 2 saddles, taking care not to pierce the meat. Sprinkle the inside of the meat with the rosemary, salt and pepper. Mix together with chopped garlic and the olives, then spread the mixture down the centre of each saddle. Roll up the meat, taking care to roll tightly and neatly, then secure the 2 rolls of stuffed meat with thin kitchen string.

Heat the olive oil in a frying pan and briskly seal the rolls on all sides until golden brown. Add the tomatoes, stock and tomato juice to the pan, stirring well to mix. Season with salt and pepper, cover and cook over a moderate heat for 20 minutes. Check the level of the liquid in the pan frequently, stirring and shaking the ingredients from time to time. After 20 minutes, remove the rolls to a hot plate and allow the remaining sauce to reduce and thicken. Serve sliced, on the tomato sauce.

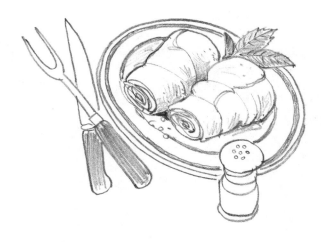

QUAIL SALAD

Quail are popular in Italy. Here the freshly cooked meat is added to a prepared salad and served with a warm dressing.

Serves 4

INGREDIENTS
4 fresh quail
4 small servings of mixed green
  salad
5 tbsps oil
½ carrot, chopped
1 shallot, chopped
Salt and freshly ground black
  pepper
1 tbsp olive oil
Vinegar
4 slices of white bread

Remove the legs and the breast meat from the quail. Draw the bird if this has not been done by the butcher and discard all the entrails. Wash the salad greens and dry the leaves well.

Heat 1 tbsp oil in a pan and add the wings and the carcases. brown well and cover with 280ml/½ pint water. Add the carrot and shallot, and season with salt and pepper. Leave on a high heat until the stock has reduced by half. Strain the stock through a fine sieve and discard the bones. Put the stock back on a high heat and cook until it becomes quite syrupy. Remove from the heat and allow to cool. Once the stock has cooled, stir in the olive oil and a drop of vinegar. Stir well and set aside.

Cut the sliced bread into small cubes. Heat 2 tbsps of oil in a frying pan and fry the cubes on all sides. Drain on absorbent kitchen paper when golden, then add to the salad. Season the quail meat and legs with lots of salt and pepper and sauté in the remaining oil until cooked through completely. Serve the legs and quail meat immediately on a bed of salad with the sauce poured over.

211

ROAST QUAIL

Quail are small and cook very quickly. Do not overcook these tiny birds or they will become dry.

Serves 4

INGREDIENTS

4 large quail, drawn
1 tbsp freshly chopped rosemary
1 tbsp oil
Salt and freshly ground black pepper

Preheat the oven to 220°C/425°F/Gas Mark 7. Cut off and discard the wing tips and legs of the quail. Rinse the birds under cold running water. Sprinkle with insides of the quail evenly with the rosemary, and salt and pepper. Tie the quail up neatly with thin kitchen string.

Heat the oil in a frying pan and seal the quail on all sides, then transfer to a roasting tin and cook for 20-25 minutes until crisp and golden.

PARTRIDGE 'GOURMET CLUB'

This is truly a dish for gourmets, containing some wonderful ingredients including goose liver and truffles. Don't overcook the partridge – they dry out very easily.

Serves 8

INGREDIENTS

340g/12oz white beans (or haricot beans), soaked
4 partridges
Salt and freshly ground black pepper
60g/2oz butter
5 tbsps goose liver, chopped
5 tbsps truffles, chopped
8 thin slices of pork fat
120g/4oz bacon in one piece
120g/4oz prosciutto crudo
2 tbsps olive oil
430ml/¾ pint chopped tomato pulp or passata

Boil beans in unsalted water until tender, about 2 hours. Split the partridges in half, then flatten the halves slightly by pounding gently. Remove and discard the smallest bones, then season the meat with salt and pepper. Heat the butter in a large frying pan. Brown the partridge halves on both sides, then drain and allow to cool. Stuff the halves with chopped goose liver and truffle, and wrap in pork fat. Return the partridges to the pan juices and continue sautéing, turning from time to time while the beans are prepared.

Cook the bacon in boiling water for 1 hour. Remove and dice. Sauté the prosciutto in olive oil for 1 minute, then add the tomato pulp, season with salt and pepper, and simmer for 10 minutes. Add the bacon and cooked beans and heat through. Place the partridges on a warmed platter, pour the pan juices over and serve with the beans.

CALVES' LIVER VENETIAN STYLE

Calves' liver adds more than a touch of luxury to this simple but sumptuous dish, but lambs' liver may be used as an alternative.

Serves 4

INGREDIENTS
225g/8oz onion, sliced
60ml/2 fl oz olive oil
57-g/1¾lbs calves' liver
Salt and freshly ground black
  pepper
2 lemons, cut into wedges

Fry the onions in the oil until golden brown, stirring constantly. Cut the liver into thin slices, removing membranes and other tough portions. Season with freshly ground pepper and add to pan. Cook for 3-4 minutes until brown on both sides. Sprinkle with salt and turn out onto a hot serving plate. Garnish with lemon wedges.

BRAISED OXTAIL COWHERD STYLE

Oxtail is rich, unctious and one of my favourite winter foods. Serve with potatoes mashed with olive oil, or polenta.

Serves 6

INGREDIENTS
1 oxtail, weighing about
    2kg/4½lbs
2 bay leaves
2 carrots, chopped
1 head celery, sliced
225g/8oz lean bacon, chopped
120g/4oz prosciutto crudo,
    chopped
1 onion, chopped
225ml/8 fl oz white wine
460ml/16 fl oz passata
Beef stock
Pinch powdered cinnamon
Salt and freshly ground black
    pepper

Cut the oxtail into pieces and soak them in a pan of cold water for at least 2 hours. Bring the water to a boil with a bouquet garni consisting of bay leaves, 1 of the carrots and a handful of the celery. Boil the oxtail for 1 hour, skimming occasionally, then drain.

Sauté the bacon, prosciutto crudo, remaining carrot and onion until golden. Add the oxtail and brown for 10 minutes, then pour in the wine and simmer until it evaporates. Add the passata to the pan. Cover and continue cooking for about 3 hours over low heat, adding a little stock as necessary. Dice the remaining celery and cook for 10 minutes in boiling salted water. Drain and add to oxtail about ½ hour before completion of cooking. Season with a pinch of cinnamon, salt and a little freshly ground pepper just before serving.

DESSERTS, ICES & BISCUITS

When I was a child we had just one family holiday abroad and that was to Italy. We stayed in a riviera resort, admittedly not the best place to form an authoritative opinion of classic Italian cookery, and the only thing that I remember about the desserts served to us in the hotel was the stunning bowls of fresh fruit, especially the peaches. They were served in iced water and were huge, ripe and incredibly juicy. I wasn't really at all interested in food at that time and my only other culinary remembrance is of the delicious ice creams that you could buy simply everywhere!

How things change! Mention Italian food to me now and, although I generally prefer savoury foods, I will start thinking of, and drooling over, the wonderful array of Italian desserts.

Glorious Italian Gelati!

I think I must start by being lyrical about ice cream. Gone are the days when the image of ice cream revolved around a cornet or a wafer to lick tentatively in hot weather. Ice cream is now a designer dessert, with vanilla flavouring giving way to rich vanilla in an attempt to make it sound more interesting next to such exotic varieties as pistachio, cherry, honey and caramel.

I have been unable to track down the origins of ice cream making in Italy. Most authorities acknowledge that it was made in China from around 2,000 BC but that the Italians did not begin their famous tradition of ice cream making until the seventeenth century. It is therefore safe to assume that Marco Polo was unable to return to Italy with any samples in his freezer bag following his travels to the Orient in the late thirteenth century! It is, however, certain that a Sicilian, one Francesco Procopio dei Coltelli (Procope to his friends, and to most food historians!) introduced both ice creams and sorbets to Paris society through his coffee house in the French capital in around 1670.

Italian ice creams are of two types – gelati, which are milk based ices or granitas, which are more like sorbets and strongly flavoured, sometimes with fruit but traditionally with coffee. Included within this chapter are some wonderful Italian ice cream recipes – one of my favourites is the Honey Ice Cream with Pine Nuts. I suggest you use the best and most fragrant flower honey that you can find to make the ice cream as flavoursome as possible.

Cassata – Sponge or Ice Cream?

Cassata is one of the best known of Italian desserts but there seems to be some confusion over what it is! Thumbing through copious recipe books has brought me to the conclusion that *Sicilian* cassata is a rich sponge cake, usually laced with alcohol and iced with a rich chocolate frosting, whereas cassata is generally a layered ice cream, frequently containing glacé fruits. Larousse Gastronomique, the culinary bible, warns that cassata varies greatly in quality and delicacy – hardly surprising when it is two different things!

Two Great Orange Desserts

I don't immediately associate Italy with oranges but two Italian orange desserts are now justly popular throughout the world. One is Caramel Oranges where the bitterness or darkness of the caramel can easily be adjusted to suit your own individual taste. There is one secret to success in preparing this dish – a very sharp serrated edged knife for peeling the oranges. This will remove every last trace of the bitter white pith from the fruit and will also enable you to cut the oranges neatly into slices which will keep their shape and texture until they are served.

The second dessert is Frozen Oranges. These are now available, commercially prepared, in supermarkets and specialist food stores, but nothing can match the flavour of a home-made orange sorbet which can easily be spooned into the orange shells that have given up their fruit for the frozen dessert. Filling the shells may take a while so, especially if you have guests, I would suggest filling the oranges and returning them to the freezer until required. To ensure that the oranges look as attractive as possible, do not fill the shells until about 30 minutes before you are expecting your guests – I never think that they look quite so good if they have been completely frozen.

Finally, I would recommend the delicious Piedmont Pear Pie. It has a most unusual pastry which includes the typical Italian ingredient of cornmeal, more commonly used for making cornbread or, finely ground, for making polenta. Remember that Italian pears are large and use extra fruit if necessary. I have served this recipe to friends who are great gastronomes with considerable success – and a rich chocolate sauce!

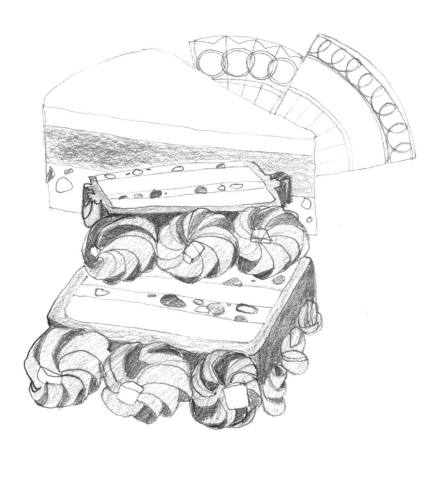

TIMBALLO CON LE PERE ALLA PIEMONTESE – PIEDMONT PEAR PIE

A traditional pear pie from Piedmont in north west Italy, flavoured with cloves and red wine, and with an interesting pastry containing cornmeal.

Serves 4-6

INGREDIENTS
For Pie-crust
225g/8oz plain flour
Salt
90g/3oz yellow cornmeal
175g/6oz caster sugar
120g/4oz butter
3 egg yolks

For Filling
6 large firm cooking pears,
    peeled
120g/4oz sugar
150ml/¼ pint red wine
1 whole clove
Pinch cinnamon

Preheat the oven to 190°C/375°F/Gas Mark 5. Place the pears in a saucepan with the sugar, wine, clove, and cinnamon. Simmer for 15 minutes or until pears are almost tender. Cool.

Mix the flour, a pinch of salt, cornmeal and sugar together in a bowl. Rub in 100g/3½oz of the butter until the mixture resembles fine breadcrumbs. Stir in the egg yolks and, if necessary, a little water to make a stiff dough. Knead a few times on a floured surface until a smooth ball, then rest, covered, for 30 minutes.

Roll out two thirds of the pastry and use to line the bottom and sides of 20cm/8 inch pie dish. Drain and pears and place in the lined pie dish.

Roll out the remaining pastry and place over the filling. Dampen and crimp the edges to seal, and make a small slit in the top of the pie. Bake in the preheated oven until well browned and crisp, about 35-40 minutes. Serve hot.

ZUPPA INGLESE

Not so much a soup, more an Italian interpretation of a classic English trifle, with a rich thick custard, and strawberries.

Serves 6-8

INGREDIENTS
30g/1oz cornflour
570ml/1 pint milk
2 eggs, lightly beaten
30g/1oz sugar
Grated rind of ½ a lemon
Pinch of nutmeg
1 punnet ripe strawberries
16 sponge fingers or boudoir
  biscuits
Amaretto
150ml/¼ pint double cream

Mix the cornflour with a little of the milk. Beat the eggs, sugar, lemon rind and nutmeg together and pour in the remaining milk. Mix with the cornflour mixture in a heavy-based pan and stir over gentle heat until the mixture thickens and comes to the boil. Allow to boil for 1 minute or until the mixture coats the back of a spoon. Place a sheet of greaseproof paper directly on top of the custard and allow it to cool slightly.

Save 8 even-sized strawberries for garnish and hull the remaining ones. Place half of the sponge fingers in the bottom of a glass bowl and sprinkle with some Amaretto. Cut the strawberries in half and place a layer on top of the sponge fingers. Pour a layer of custard on top and repeat with the remaining sliced strawberries and sponge fingers. Top with another layer of custard and allow to cool completely.

Whip the cream and spread a thin layer over the top of the set custard. Pipe the remaining cream around the edge of the dish and decorate with the reserved strawberries. Serve chilled.

ALMOND-STUFFED FIGS

Figs have always been popular in Italy and there are many references to them from Roman times. This makes a simple but special dessert.

Serves 4

INGREDIENTS
4 large ripe figs
4 tbsps ground almonds
2 tbsps orange juice
2 tbsps finely chopped dried
  apricots
4 tbsps natural yogurt
Finely grated rind ½ orange
Wedges of figs and mint, or
  strawberry leaves for
  decoration

Cut each fig into four quarters using a sharp knife, but do not cut right down through the base. Ease the four sections of each fig outward to form a flower shape.

Place the ground almonds, orange juice and chopped apricots in a small bowl and mix together thoroughly. Divide the mixture into four, and press it into the centre of each fig.

Make a sauce by mixing the yogurt with the orange rind, then thin it down with just a little water or orange juice. Spoon a small pool of orange yogurt onto each of four plates, and sit a stuffed fig into the centre of each pool. Decorate with the additional wedges of fig, and the mint or strawberry leaves.

APPLE FRITTERS

Serve these fritters with a fresh fruit coulis – raspberry or plum work well – or with an egg custard.

Serves 4

INGREDIENTS
2 Golden Delicious apples, peeled, cored and cut into small pieces
120ml/4 fl oz orange juice
60ml/2 fl oz Marsala
225g/8oz self raising-flour, sifted
30g/1oz ground almonds
2 egg yolks
60g/2oz sugar
120ml/4 fl oz milk
Oil for deep-frying

Marinate the apples in the orange juice and Marsala for 15 minutes. Mix together the flour and the ground almonds. Whisk together the egg yolks and sugar until quite white. Beat together the egg mixture and the flour mixture. Stir in the milk and beat thoroughly. Add the flour and egg mixture to the apples in their marinade. Stir gently to blend the ingredients together then allow to rest for 10 minutes.

Heat the oil and carefully add spoonfuls of the mixture. Allow to cook through and turn golden brown, then remove with a slotted spoon. Drain on kitchen paper and serve either hot or cold.

GNOCCHI WITH PRUNE FILLING

Gnocchi are usually savory, but they are just as delicious with a sweet filling.

Serves 4

INGREDIENTS
460g/1lb potatoes, steamed in
  their skins
½ egg, beaten
1 tbsp milk
60g/2oz butter
120g/4oz flour
Sugar
Cinnamon
24 prunes, pitted
3 tbsps Eau de Vie (fruit
  flavoured alcohol)

Peel the steamed potatoes and dry them on kitchen paper. Push the potatoes through a fine sieve. Beat the egg, milk and 30g/1oz of butter into the potatoes. Mix well and then add the flour, beating constantly. Once well mixed, form the dough into a ball.

Sprinkle a little sugar and cinnamon into each of the prunes. With floured fingers, break off a little gnocchi dough to wrap around each prune, making sure that the dough is well sealed around the prunes. Bring a large saucepan of water to the boil, add the gnocchi and cook them until they rise to the surface. Remove with a slotted spoon and set aside to dry on a clean tea towel.

Heat the remaining butter in a frying pan and sauté the gnocchi, sprinkling over more sugar and cinnamon to taste. Pour the Eau de Vie over and serve.

ACACIA BLOOM FRITTERS

The acacia tree blooms in May and the flowers make splendid fritters. Try this if you can obtain the flowers – a similar dish can be made with elderflowers.

Serves 4

INGREDIENTS
225g/8oz flour, sifted
1 tsp salt
120ml/4 fl oz lager beer
200ml/7 fl oz water
1 tbsp fruit-flavoured alcohol
1 tbsp melted butter
2 egg whites
200ml/7 fl oz oil
16 acacia flowers
Sugar for dredging

Whisk together the flour, salt, beer and warm water, then whisk in the alcohol and melted butter. Beat in the egg whites stiffly and fold them gently into the mixture.

Heat the oil in a pan. Dip the acacia flowers in the batter and then fry them in the medium hot oil, turning them until they are golden brown all over. Drain on kitchen paper and dredge with sugar. Serve hot.

PESCHE IN TEGAME –
BAKED STUFFED PEACHES

Wonderfully juicy peaches are grown in Italy. This recipe for baked peaches has an unusual filling flavoured with bitter cocoa. Peaches are easy to skin by plunging them into boiling water, in the same way as tomatoes.

Serves 4

INGREDIENTS
4 large firm but ripe peaches
120g/4oz sugar
Grated rind of 1 lemon
2 tbsps bitter cocoa
45g/1½oz blanched almonds, chopped
5 bitter almond macaroons, crumbled
1 egg yolk
Peach liqueur
2 tbsps butter

Preheat the oven to 180°C/350°F/Gas Mark 4. Peel the peaches. Split in half and remove the stones. Scoop out some of the peach leaving a shell 2.5cm/1 inch thick. Place the peach flesh in a bowl with half the sugar, the lemon rind, cocoa, almonds, macaroons and egg yolk. Mix with enough liqueur to form a thick paste. Stuff the peach halves with this filling, then arrange them in a baking dish. Dot with butter, sprinkle with the remaining sugar and bake in the preheated oven for 25-30 minutes, or until peaches are tender and still hold their shape.

CASSATE ALLA SICILIANA – SICILIAN CHEESECAKE

Ricotta cheese, one of the most versatile of Italian cheeses, is my favourite for making cheesecakes, with its mild, very slightly acid flavour.

Serves 6

INGREDIENTS
680g/1½lbs Ricotta cheese, sieved
225g/8oz sugar
Triple sec liqueur
120g/4oz bitter chocolate, coarsely grated
90g/3oz chopped candied fruits
Boudoir biscuits
Cognac

Mix the Ricotta and sugar until creamy. Remove about 120g/4oz and set aside for the top of the cake. Add 1 tbsp of liqueur to the remaining cheese along with chocolate and candied fruits. Chill the mixture for 30 minutes.

Line a loaf tin with waxed paper. Mix equal parts cognac and liqueur, then dip the boudoir biscuits in the mixture and use to line the bottom and sides of the loaf tin. Spoon the Ricotta mixture into the tin, pressing it down and levelling it with a spatula. Cover with more boudoirs moistened with the cognac-liqueur mixture. Chill for a few hours.

When ready to serve, turn the cassata out upside down on a platter, if it doesn't come out easily, immerse the tin briefly in boiling water. Remove the wax paper, cover the cassata with the reserved Ricotta and serve sliced.

ZABAGLIONE

I remember the first time that I tasted zabaglione in a flat in Bayswater with some Hungarians! Nothing at all to do with Italy, except that Zabaglione is the classic Italian dessert!

Serves 4

INGREDIENTS
4 egg yolks
4 tablespoons caster sugar
4 tablespoons Marsala wine
Sponge fingers to serve

Place all the ingredients in a large heatproof bowl. Beat with a balloon whisk until light and frothy. Stand the bowl over a pan of water over a low heat and continue to whisk. The mixture will froth and is now ready to serve immediately with sponge fingers. An instant Italian desert, but do not overheat or the mixture will curdle and not become frothy.

RICOTTA PANCAKES WITH HONEY AND RAISIN SAUCE

Cheese, honey and raisins may sound a strange mixture to serve with pancakes but these are delicious. Definitely my favourite way of eating pancakes!

Serves 4

INGREDIENTS
Sauce
4 tbsps clear honey
Juice of ½ lemon
1 tbsp raisins
1 tbsp pine kernels

Filling
225g/8oz Ricotta cheese
Grated rind of ½ lemon
2 tbsps raisins
1 tsp chopped pine kernels
8 small, hot pancakes

To decorate
Twists of lemon

To make the sauce, put all the ingredients into a small pan and warm through gently. For the filling, beat the cheese and the lemon rind until soft; mix in the raisins and pine kernels. Divide the filling among the hot pancakes and either roll them up or fold them into triangles. Arrange the pancakes on warm plates, spoon the sauce over the top and decorate with twists of lemon. Serve immediately.

ZUPPA ALLA ROMANA

This is a rich Italian trifle flavoured with orange and Curaçao. Don't eat too much!

Serves 6

INGREDIENTS
1 large sponge cake, sliced
6 tbsps apricot jam
120ml/4 fl oz Curaçao
430ml/¾ pint cold, thick custard
280ml/½ pint double cream
3 tsps icing sugar
Toasted flaked almonds
Crystallised orange peel cut into
  strips

Line the bottom of a glass serving dish with half the cake. Sprinkle half the Curaçao over the cake. Spread the jam on top and cover with the remaining slices, then pour the remaining Curaçao over. Spoon the custard over the cake. Whip the cream and gradually add the icing sugar until it peaks. Spoon the cream over the custard and decorate with lightly toasted flaked almonds and strips of candied orange peel.

MARSALA CREAM

This is a rich creamy dessert which is flavoured with Marsala, a sweet Italian fortified wine. Use sherry if Marsala is not available.

Serves 6

INGREDIENTS
340ml/12 fl oz double cream
4 tbsps sugar
3 tbsps Marsala
4 tbsps honey
3 tbsps lemon juice
3 egg whites
Soft brown sugar
1 packet Amaretti biscuits

Whip the cream, adding the sugar gradually. Fold in the Marsala, honey and lemon juice. Beat the egg whites until stiff and fold into the cream. Spoon into individual glass serving dishes. Decorate with brown sugar and crumbled Amaretti biscuits.

SPONGE CAKE WITH ORANGE AND LEMON ZEST

A light, bright sponge cake, ideal for an afternoon snack, or for serving with fresh fruit or custard.

Serves 4

INGREDIENTS
90g/3oz sugar
90g/3oz butter, softened at room
 temperature
2 eggs, separated
90g/3oz self-raising flour, sifted
4 tbsps cornflour, sifted
Pinch of salt
1 tbsp orange and lemon zest,
 blanched and drained
Flour for dredging
Butter for greasing

Preheat the oven to 190°C/375°F/Gas Mark 5. Grease and flour a 20cm/8 inch deep, round cake tin. Whisk the sugar, butter and egg yolks together for a few minutes. Gradually whisk the flour, cornflour and a pinch of salt into the mixture, beating continuously. Stir in the orange and lemon zests. Beat the egg whites until very stiff, then gently fold them into the cake mixture.

Spoon the mixture into the prepared cake tin and bake in a hot oven for approximately 35 minutes. Serve warm or cold.

CARAMEL ORANGES

This dessert is so internationally popular that I was surprised to find that it is Italian! Whatever its origins, it is always popular.

Serves 4

INGREDIENTS
4 large oranges
300g/11oz sugar
340ml/12 fl oz water
60ml/2 fl oz extra water
2 tbsps brandy or orange liqueur

Use a swivel vegetable peeler to peel thin strips of zest from two of the oranges. Take off any white pith and cut the pieces into very thin julienne strips with a sharp knife. Place the julienne strips in a small saucepan, cover with water and bring to the boil. Drain.

Peel all the oranges with a serrated-edged knife. Cut the ends off first and then take the peel and pith off in very thin strips using a sawing motion. Cut the oranges horizontally into slices about 6mm/¼ inch thick. Combine the sugar and water in a heavy-based pan, reserving the extra 60ml/2 fl oz water for later use. Place the mixture over medium heat until the sugar has dissolved. Add the drained orange peel strips to the pan. Boil the syrup gently, uncovered, for about 10 minutes or until the orange strips are glazed. Remove the strips from the pan and place on a lightly oiled plate.

Return the pan to a high heat and allow the syrup to boil, uncovered, until it turns a pale golden brown. Remove from the heat immediately and quickly but carefully add the extra water. Return to gentle heat and cook for a few minutes to dissolve any hardened sugar. Remove the pan from the heat and allow it to cool completely. Stir in the brandy.

Arrange the orange slices in a serving dish then pour over the cooled syrup. Pile the glazed orange strips on top and refrigerate the oranges for several hours, or overnight, before serving.

MONTEBIANCO CON MARRONS GLACÉS – MONT BLANC WITH MARRONS GLACÉS

Italy produces most of the marrons glacés devoured throughout Europe at Christmas time. This sweet confection of chestnuts is a perfect Christmas dessert.

Serves 6-8

INGREDIENTS
1.15kg/2½lbs chestnuts
Milk
1 tsp vanilla essence
Sugar to taste
280ml/½ pint double cream,
  whipped
Marrons glacés

Slit the chestnuts, place them in a pan and cover with water. Boil for about 30 minutes, then drain and peel, removing both shell and brown inner skin. Cover the chestnuts with milk in a saucepan. Add the vanilla and bring to the boil. Cover and cook over a low heat for about 45 minutes or until chestnuts are tender and mealy. Stir occasionally to prevent sticking. Drain the chestnuts and beat them to a purée. Weigh the purée and add half the amount of sugar. Cook the purée over a moderate heat and, stirring frequently, cook until the mixture becomes thick and pulls away from sides of saucepan, about 30 minutes. Remove from the heat and cool completely. Press the chestnuts through a potato ricer, letting them fall in a mound on a serving plate. Cover this with whipped cream and garnish with marrons glacés. Chill until ready to serve.

MARSALA ICE CREAM TORTE

Not only do the Italians make excellent ice cream – they also make delicious ice cream cakes – try it!

Serves 6-8

INGREDIENTS
Oil for greasing
3 egg whites
225g/8oz sugar
1 tbsp instant coffee
2 tbsps boiling water
420ml/¾ pint cream
2 tbsps Marsala
280ml/½ pint chocolate ice
  cream, softened
Grated chocolate or cocoa and
  whipped cream to decorate

Preheat the oven to
150°C/300°F/Gas Mark 2. Lightly
oil a baking sheet and line the
base of a 20cm/8 inch round,
loose-bottomed cake tin with
greaseproof paper. Whisk the
egg whites, gradually add the
sugar and continue to whisk until
stiff. Add the remaining sugar
and whisk until the mixture
peaks. Fill a piping bag fitted
with a star nozzle with the
meringue mixture. Pipe small
rosettes onto the baking sheet,
keeping them well apart. Bake in
a preheated oven for 1 hour,
then leave in the oven for a
further 20 minutes with the heat
turned off. Remove the
meringues from the oven and
allow them to cool.

Mix the coffee with the water in
a small bowl. Whip the cream
until thick, then fold in all but 4
of the meringues. Add the coffee
and the Marsala, taking care not
to crush the meringues. Fold in
the ice cream. Use the mixture to
fill the prepared cake tin. Cover
and freeze until firm. Put the
reserved meringues in the centre
of the torte and decorate the top
with piped whipped cream and
grated chocolate or cocoa if
wished. Remove from the freezer
to the refrigerator 10-15 minutes
before serving.

PRUNE ICE CREAM

A simple-to-make, rich-tasting ice cream

Serves 4

INGREDIENTS
250ml/8 fl oz egg custard (see
  Banana Ice Cream recipe)
10 prunes, stoned
1 squeeze lemon juice

Process the prunes with the lemon juice in a food processor. The prunes will form a thick dark paste. Put this prune paste in a large bowl and pour over the egg custard. Blend with a hand mixer until quite smooth. Pour into the bowl of an ice cream maker and set the machine in motion. Once the ice cream has 'taken', spoon into a container and keep in the freezer until needed. If an ice cream maker is not available, part freeze the mixture, whisk and refreeze. Whisk the mixture again until smooth and creamy, then pour into a covered container and freeze until firm.

CASSATA

This is one of the most famous Italian ice creams. Its dramatic, layered presentation makes it a stunning dinner party dessert. Remove the cling film between each layer but always keep the top surface covered in the freezer!

Serves 6-8

INGREDIENTS
Almond Layer
2 eggs, separated
60g/2oz icing sugar
150ml/¼ pint double cream
½ tsp almond essence

Chocolate Layer
2 eggs, separated
60g/2oz icing sugar
150ml/¼ pint double bream
60g/2oz plain chocolate
30g/1oz cocoa
1½ tbsps water

Fruit Layer
280ml/½ pint double cream
2 tbsps maraschino or light rum
1 egg white
60g/2oz icing sugar
60g/2oz mixed glacé fruits
30g/1oz shelled chopped
  pistachios

To prepare the almond layer, beat the egg whites until stiff peaks form, gradually beating in the icing sugar, a spoonful at a time. Lightly beat the egg yolks and fold in the whites. Whip the cream with the almond essence until soft peaks form, then fold it into the egg mixture. Lightly oil a 20cm/8 inch round cake tin. Pour in the almond mixture and smooth over the top. Cover with clingfilm and freeze until firm. Remove the film.

To prepare the chocolate layer, beat the egg whites until stiff but not dry, then gradually beat in the icing sugar. Whip the cream until soft and fold in the egg white mixture. Put the chocolate in the top of a double boiler or a bowl over simmering water and heat until melted. Remove it from the heat and stir in the egg yolks. Combine the cocoa and water and add them to the chocolate mixture. Allow to cool and then fold it into the egg whites. Spoon the chocolate layer over the almond layer and return, covered with film to the freezer. Remove the film when frozen.

To make the rum fruit layer, whip the cream until soft peaks form. Whisk the egg white until about the same consistency as the cream. Gradually add the icing sugar, beating well after each addition. Combine the two mixtures, then fold in the rum, fruit and nuts. Spread this mixture on top of the chocolate layer, cover and freeze until firm.

To serve, loosen the cassata from around the edges of the pan with a small knife. Place a hot cloth around the pan for a few seconds to help. Turn out onto a serving plate and cut into wedges to serve.

AMARENA ICE CREAM

Amarena is an Italian cherry – I always think that Italian cherries have the best flavour. They make wonderful ice cream.

Serves 4

INGREDIENTS
6 egg yolks
120g/4oz sugar
520ml/18 fl oz milk
4 tbsps canned Amarena cherries, in their juice, roughly chopped

Whisk together the egg yolks and the sugar until the mixture becomes pale. Bring the milk to the boil and whisk it into the egg mixture. Rinse the pan, return the custard to it and heat gently, whisking continuously, until the mixture thickens. Remove from the heat and stir in the chopped Amarena cherries and their juice.

Pour into the bowl of an ice cream maker and freeze. Spoon into a container once the ice cream has crystallized, and keep in the freezer until needed. Alternatively, pour the mixture into a bowl and place in the freezer until partly frozen. Remove the bowl from the freezer and whisk the mixture. Refreeze, whisk thoroughly, and pour into a covered container. Freeze until firm.

HONEY ICE CREAM WITH PINE NUTS

I often make an ice cream with honey and cardamoms – this is a wonderful variation on a family favourite. Use a scented, clear honey.

Serves 4

INGREDIENTS
2 tbsps clear honey
6 egg yolks
520ml/18 fl oz milk
30g/1oz pine nuts

Whisk the honey and the egg yolks together for 1 minute. Bring the milk to the boil, and pour over the egg mixture, whisking continuously. Rinse the saucepan and pour the mixture back into the pan, add the pine nuts and place over a very low heat. Stir continuously, until the custard thickens and will coat the back of a spoon.

Allow to cool and then pour into the bowl of an ice cream maker and freeze. Spoon into a container and keep in the freezer until needed. Alternatively, part freeze the mixture in a bowl, whisk until smooth then refreeze. Whisk again and freeze in a covered container until firm.

STRAWBERRY ICE CREAM

When I make strawberry ice cream I always leave the fruit in chunks, to prove that it is home-made!

Serves 4

INGREDIENTS
300ml/11 fl oz egg custard (see Banana Ice Cream)
150g/5oz strawberries, washed and hulled
60ml/2 fl oz single cream

Prepare the egg custard as in the recipe for Banana Ice Cream. Either chop the strawberries into small pieces and mix them into the egg custard, or add them whole to the custard and blend until smooth with a hand mixer, or in a liquidiser or food processor. Stir in the cream and pour into the bowl of an ice cream maker, and freeze. When the ice cream has 'taken', spoon into a container and keep in the freezer until needed.
Alternatively, part freeze the mixture in a bowl, then whisk and refreeze. Whisk again, pour into a covered container and freeze until firm.

CHOCOLATE ICE CREAM

This is a typical Italian chocolate ice cream – smooth and rich!

Serves 4

INGREDIENTS
120g/4oz sugar
6 egg yolks
520ml/18 fl oz milk
4 tbsps cocoa powder
(unsweetened)

Whisk the sugar and egg yolks together until the mixture becomes thick and pale. Bring the milk to boil in a large saucepan, and whisk it into the egg mixture. Rinse the pan and return the custard to it. Whisk continuously over a low heat until the mixture thickens. Once the sauce is thick, remove from the heat and stir in the chocolate powder.

Pour the mixture into the bowl of an ice cream maker and freeze. Once the ice cream has crystallized it can be spooned into a container and kept in the freezer until needed. Alternatively, pour the mixture into a bowl and place in the freezer until mushy. Remove bowl from freezer and whisk the mixture. Refreeze, whisk thoroughly, pour into a covered container and freeze until firm.

CARAMEL ICE CREAM

Caramel is such a versatile flavouring and it makes wonderful ice cream, served with a caramel sauce.

Serves 4

INGREDIENTS
3 egg yolks
150g/5oz sugar
250ml/9 fl oz milk
150ml/¼ pint water
2 tbsps double cream

Whisk the egg yolks with 30g/1oz of the sugar until the mixture becomes pale. Bring the milk to the boil and pour it onto the egg mixture, whisking continuously. Rinse the pan, return the custard to it and continue cooking over a low heat until a thick egg custard is reached, stirring continuously. Remove from the heat and set aside.

Place the remaining sugar in a small saucepan with 3 tablespoons of water and cook over a high heat until a caramel forms. Remove from the heat and carefully stir in the remaining water. Place back over a very low heat, stirring well so that the water is thoroughly mixed into the caramel. Allow to warm through. Mix three quarters of the caramel into the egg custard. Pour this into the bowl of the ice cream maker and freeze. Alternatively, pour the caramel-custard mixture into a bowl and place in the freezer until part frozen. Remove from the freezer, whisk and refreeze. Whisk thoroughly until smooth, then pour into a covered container and freeze until firm.

To make the sauce, mix the cream into the remaining caramel and stir well. Serve the ice cream with the caramel sauce poured over.

BANANA ICE CREAM

The Italians are great ice cream makers. For a true Italian flavour, add a spoonful or two of rum.

Serves 4

INGREDIENTS
4 egg yolks
45g/1½oz caster sugar
300ml/11 fl oz milk
225g/8oz bananas, prepared weight
Few drops lemon juice

Whisk the egg yolks and sugar together until pale and thick. Heat the milk until almost boiling, then pour it over the eggs, stirring constantly. Rinse the pan, return the custard to it and stir the custard over a low heat until it thickens.

Mash the banana with a fork and add a few drops of lemon juice. Add to the egg custard and blend until smooth with a hand mixer. Pour into the bowl of an ice cream maker and freeze. Alternatively, pour the mixture into a bowl and place in the freezer until part frozen. Remove from the freezer and whisk. Refreeze and whisk thoroughly until smooth. Pour into a covered container and replace in the freezer until required.

FROZEN ORANGES

Commercially prepared sorbets in orange shells are now available, but they simply do not compare to home-made!

Serves 4

INGREDIENTS
Approximately 6 oranges to give
   300ml/11 fl oz orange juice
150ml/¼ pint water
150g/5oz sugar

Cut the tops off the oranges and remove the pulp with the help of a small spoon, keeping the orange skins whole. Squeeze the juice from the pulp and measure it – you need 300ml/11 fl oz of freshly squeezed orange juice – you may require more oranges to make up this quantity.

Mix together the orange juice, water and sugar with a whisk, then pour into an ice cream maker. Set the machine in motion. When the sorbet is crystallized, spoon it back into the orange skins and freeze until required. Alternatively, place the mixture in a shallow container and freeze until mushy. Gently break up with a fork, refreeze and spoon into the chilled orange 'shells' to serve.

244

RHUBARB SORBET

I sometimes flavour this with a little grated lime zest and juice – it makes a very refreshing sorbet.

Serves 4

INGREDIENTS
460g/1lb rhubarb
340ml/12 fl oz water
175g/6oz sugar

Peel the rhubarb and cut into small pieces. Place in a saucepan with the water and sugar. Bring to the boil and cook for 5 minutes. Blend until smooth in a liquidiser or food processor, then pour into the bowl of an ice cream maker. Set the machine in motion and stop when the sorbet is crystallized. Spoon into a container and keep in the freezer until needed. Alternatively, part freeze the mixture in a shallow container, break up gently with a fork and then pour into a covered container and freeze until needed.

GELATO DI LIMONE – LEMON WATER ICE

Water ices are very refreshing and are almost as popular in Italy as ice creams. They are very easy to make – use un-waxed lemons for this recipe if possible.

Serves 4-6

INGREDIENTS
1 litre/1¾ pints water
460g/1lb sugar
Juice and grated zest of 5 lemons

Heat the water and sugar over a moderate heat for 5 minutes to dissolve the sugar. Bring to the boil for 5 minutes, then allow to cool.

Add the grated lemon zests to the syrup, together with the lemon juice. Stir well and leave for 30 minutes. Strain, pour into a container and freeze until the ice starts to set. Beat well and return to the freezer. Remove from the freezer 10-15 minutes before serving.

HAZELNUT FLORENTINES

Florentines are crisp toffee-like biscuits. This recipe uses
hazelnuts as a change from almonds – both are delicious.

Makes 24-30

INGREDIENTS
460g/1lb shelled and peeled
  hazelnuts
225g/8oz sugar
6 tbsps honey
6 tbsps double cream
225g/8oz butter
175g/6oz white chocolate, melted
175g/6oz plain chocolate, melted

Preheat the oven to
190°C/375°F/Gas Mark 5. Oil two
heavy baking sheets. Place the
hazelnuts in a plastic bag and tie
securely. Tap the nuts or roll
them with a rolling pin to crush
them roughly.

Place the sugar, honey, cream
and butter in a heavy-based
saucepan and heat gently to
dissolve the sugar. Bring to the
boil and cook rapidly for about
1½ minutes. Remove the pan

from the heat and stir in the nuts.
Spoon no more than six amounts
of mixture on to each baking
sheet, allowing room for
spreading. Bake for about 10
minutes in the preheated oven.
Allow the florentines to cool on
the baking sheets and, when
nearly set, loosen with a palette
knife and transfer to a wire rack
to cool completely.

When all Florentines have been
baked and cooled, melt both
chocolates separately. Spread
white chocolate on half of the
Florentines and dark chocolate
on the other half, or marble the
two if desired. Place chocolate
side uppermost to cool slightly
and then make a wavy pattern
with a fork, or swirl the
chocolate with a knife until it
sets in the desired pattern.

ALMOND AND WALNUT MACAROONS

Almond biscuits are popular throughout Italy and are delicious with ice cream. These also include walnuts, and are just a little bit different.

Serves 4-6

INGREDIENTS
Flour
150g/5oz ground almonds
150g/5oz ground walnuts
250g/9oz caster sugar
2 egg whites, stiffly beaten

Preheat the oven to 130°C/250°F/Gas Mark ½. Lightly grease and flour two baking sheets. Mix the walnuts and almonds together and add the sugar. Gently fold in the beaten egg whites, making sure that all the ingredients are well incorporated. Place the mixture in a piping bag fitted with a plain nozzle, and pipe out small, evenly sized macaroons. Bake in a very low oven for approximately 40 minutes. Allow to cool slightly then transfer to a wire cooling rack.

DATE AND PISTACHIO BISCUITS

*These delicious biscuits are rich, luxurious and different!
Shape into rounds if you do not have the boat-shaped
barquette tins.*

Makes about 12

INGREDIENTS
120g/4oz butter
60g/2oz soft brown sugar
120g/4oz wholemeal flour
60g/2oz ground almonds
90g/3oz stoned dates, chopped
2 tbsps chopped, shelled,
  pistachios

To Decorate
Chopped, shelled pistachios

Preheat the oven to
190°C/375°F/Gas Mark 5. Lightly
grease twelve barquette tins.
Work the butter, brown sugar,
flour and ground almonds to a
soft, smooth dough. Knead
lightly, working in the chopped
dates and pistachios. Press the
mixture into small boat-shaped
moulds. Press a few chopped
pistachios into the top of each
uncooked biscuit. Bake in the
oven for 12-15 minutes, then
allow to cool slightly before
transferring to a wire cooling
rack.

INDEX

A

Acacia Bloom Fritters 225
Agnello al Forno – Sicilian
  Roast Lamb 200
Arista di Maiale – Saddle of Pork
  Tuscan Style 189
Almond and Walnut Macaroons 248
Almond-stuffed Figs 222
Amarena Ice Cream 238
Anatra al Sale – Roast Duck in
  Coarse Salt 204
Anatra in Salmi – Duck Casserole 205
Apple Fritters 223
Asparagi in Forno all'Italiana –
  Baked Asparagus Italian Style 56
Aubergines Scapece 54

B

Bagna Cauda – Hot Vegetable Dip 34
Banana Ice Cream 243
Barbecued Whiting Sardinian Style 149
Basic Pasta Dough 80
Beany Lasagne 84
Beef in Barolo 197
Bistecche al Piccantino – Filet
  Mignon Piquant 196
Braised Oxtail Cowherd Style 215
Bruschetta with Tomatoes 28

C

Calabrian Oysters 136
Calamaretti alla Barese –
  Squid Bari Style 147
Calamaretti Fritti – Fried Squid 159
Calves' Liver Venetian Style 214
Cannelloni 101
Capon with Garden Vegetables 170
Caramel Ice Cream 242
Caramel Oranges 233
Carpaccio with Herbs 30
Carrettiera with Tagliatelle 96
Cassata 237
Cassate alla Siciliana –
  Sicilian Cheese Cake 227

Cheese Fondue 72
Chick Pea Salad 71
Chicken Cacciatore 168
Chicken Liver Salad 69
Chicken Livers with Peas 74
Chicken Risotto 113
Chicken Tongue Rolls 173
Chicken with Tomato Sauce 165
Chocolate Ice Cream 241
Cold Chicken Sicilian Style 167
Courgette and Pine Nut Lasagne with
  Aubergine Sauce 85
Courgette, Caper and Anchovy Salad 60
Crespelle alla Bolognese 124
Crisp-fried Sprats 160

D

Date and Pistachio Biscuits 249
Devilled Lobster Italian Style 158
Donzelline Ripiene di Accuighe –
  Anchovy Puffs 37

E

Eel in Red Wine 140
Escalopes with Cheese 178
Farfalle with Creamy Cheese Sauce 98
Finocchi al Burro con Prosciutto –
  Buttered Fennel with Ham 58

F

Fish Milanese 155
Fish Stew 148
Fresh Sardines Ligurian Style 150
Fried Courgettes and Courgette
  Flowers 50
Fried Scampi 153
Fritto Misto Mare 133
Frozen Oranges 244
Fusilli Carbonara 100

G

Gelato di Limone –
  Lemon Water Ice 246

Gnocchi with Prune Filling 224
Gnocchi with Tomato Sauce 115
Goat's Cheese Pizza 122
Goat's Cheese Salad with Tarragon 68
Gourmet Mushrooms 33
Grilled Tuna with Rosemary 137

H
Hazelnut Florentines 247
Herby Pork Chops 190
Home-made Tagliatelle with
   Summer Sauce 95
Honey Ice Cream with Pine Nuts 239

I
Individual Pizzas with Egg 123
Insalata di Riso alla Romana –
   Rice Salad Roman Style 110
Italian Salad Dressing 63

K
King Prawn Salad 135

L
Lamb Chops Calabrian 201
Lamb with Fennel 202
Lasagne 83
Livornese Fish Soup 38

M
Macaroni with Basil and
   Walnut Sauce 99
Marinated Sardines 143
Marsala Cream 231
Marsala Ice Cream Torte 235
Meat Ravioli 91
Melon and Prosciutto 27
Milanese-style Osso Buco 174
Milanese Vegetable Soup 25
Minestrone 26
Minestrone alla Milanese 35
Montebianco con Marrons Glacés –
   Mont Blanc with Marrons Glacés 234
Mozzarella Pizza 119
Mussel Risotto 107

Mussels alla Genovese 134
Mussels Marinara 131
Mutton Chops in Rich Sauce 203

O
Octopus and Squid Salad 161
Olive-stuffed Rabbit Meat 210
Onion Focaccia 76
Oseleti Scampai –
   Skewered Veal Birds 185
Osso Buco with Almond Marsala 175

P
Pappa al Pomodoro – Bread and
   Tomato Soup 36
Partridge 'Gourmet Club' 213
Pasta Shells with
   Mushroom Sauce 102
Penne with Anchovy Sauce 103
Pepper Salad with Capers 51
Pesce al Marsala – Fish with
   Marsala 145
Pesche in Tegame – Baked
   Stuffed Peaches 226
Piedmont Beef Casserole 198
Pizza Rustica 117
Poached Eggs in Barolo Sauce 73
Pollo al Latte – Chicken Cooked
   in Milk 172
Pollo con Peperoni – Chicken with
   Peppers 171
Pollo in Dolce-Forte –
   Chicken in Sweet-Sour Sauce 169
Polpette Romaine –
   Roman Meatballs 194
Pomodori Casalinghi Ripieni –
   Cook's Stuffed Tomatoes 57
Pork Roulades with Polenta 192
Potato Cakes 47
Prawn Crespelle 126
Prune Ice Cream 236

Q
Quail Salad 211

R
Rabbit and Liver Surprise 208
Ravioli with Ricotta Cheese 92

Red Mullet Salad 67
Red Mullet with Herb and
   Mushroom Sauce 156
Red Mullet with Vinaigrette Sauce 141
Rhubarb Sorbet 245
Rice Balls 109
Ricotta Pancakes with Honey and
   Raisin Sauce 229
Risi e Bisi – Rice and Peas 114
Risotto alla Milanese 111
Roast Pork Fillet with Rosemary 191
Roast Quail 212
Roman-style Artichokes 45
Romany Aubergines 48
Rosemary Chicken Surprise 166

S
Salmon Trout with Garlic Sauce 146
Sautéed Broccoli with Garlic 44
Sautéed Sliced Artichoke Hearts with
   Parsley and Garlic 43
Scaloppine alla Toscana –
   Beef Escalopes Tuscan Style 195
Seafood Pizza 121
Seafood Torta 70
Sgombro Ripieno –
   Herb Stuffed Mackerel 144
Shoulder of Veal with Truffles 179
Sicilian Caponata 31
Sicilian Ratatouille 53
Sole with Pine Nuts 151
Soufflé Pizza with Cheese 120
Spaghetti Bolognese 86
Spaghetti Marinara 87
Spaghetti with Basil and
   Tomato Sauce 88
Spaghetti with Kidney Beans
   and Pesto 89
Spaghetti with Sorrel and
   Cheese Sauce 90
Spinach Crespelle 127
Spinach Gnocchi 116
Spinach Pasta 82
Sponge Cake with Orange and
   Lemon Zest 232
Sprats in Mayonnaise 154
Stracciatella Soup 32
Strawberry Ice Cream 240
Stuffed Courgette Flowers 52
Stuffed Courgettes 75

Stuffed Mushrooms 61
Stuffed Radicchio 62
Stuffed Sardines 138
Stuffed Squid 142
Stuffed White Onions 46
Swordfish Kebabs 157

T
Tagliatelle with Bacon and
   Tomato Sauce 93
Tagliatelle with Pine Nuts 94
Tagliatelle Pescatore 97
Thyme Sorbet 29
Timballo con le Pere alla Piemontese –
   Piedmont Pear Pie 220
Tomato Salad Rustica 49
Tomato, Avocado and Mozzarella
   Salad with Basil 59
Truffle Risotto 108
Tuna and Fennel 132
Turkey Kebabs 206
Turkey Marsala 207
Tuscan-style Red Mullet 152
Tuscany Beef 199

V
Veal in Cream Sauce 182
Veal in Marjoram Sauce 180
Veal in Orange 176
Veal Marengo 177
Veal Scaloppine with Prosciutto
   and Cheese 183
Veal with Marsala Sauce 181
Vegetable Risotto 112
Vitello Tonnato – Veal with Tuna 184

W
Walnut Rabbit 209
Whelk and Cockle Salad 139
White Bean and Tuna Fish Salad 39
Wholewheat Pasta 81
Wild Mushroom Pizza 118
Winter Salami Risotto 55

Z
Zabaglione 228
Zuppa alla Romana 230
Zuppa Inglese 221